RELIGION AND SPORTS

RELIGION
AND
SPORTS
An Introduction
and Case Studies

Rebecca T. Alpert

Columbia University Press
New York

Columbia University Press
Publishers Since 1893
New York   Chichester, West Sussex
cup.columbia.edu

Library of Congress Cataloging-in-Publication Data

Alpert, Rebecca T. (Rebecca Trachtenberg), 1950–
    Religion and sports: an introduction and case studies / Rebecca T. Alpert
        pages cm
    Includes bibliographical references and index.
ISBN 978-0-231-16570-9 (cloth: acid-free paper) — ISBN 978-0-231-16571-6
(pbk.: acid-free paper) —ISBN 978-0-231-53932-6
1. Sports—Religious aspects.   I. Title.

GV706.42.A56   2015
796.01—dc23   2014039573

Columbia University Press books are printed on permanent and
durable acid-free paper.

This book is printed on paper with recycled content.
Printed in the United States of America

c 10 9 8 7 6 5 4 3 2 1
p 10 9 8 7 6 5 4 3 2 1

COVER DESIGN BY JULIA KUSHNIRSKY
COVER PHOTOGRAPH: PHOTOALTO/SANDRO DI CARLO DARSA

References to Web sites (URLs) were accurate at the time of
writing. Neither the author nor Columbia University Press is
responsible for URLs that may have expired or changed since
the manuscript was prepared.

CONTENTS

A NOTE TO INSTRUCTORS ON HOW TO USE THIS TEXT

This case study book is intended as a primary or complementary text for courses in religion and sports. The introduction presents issues and background that would be covered by other texts often used in such courses.[1] What makes this book unique is the case studies. The case studies provide opportunities for students to explore these issues (e.g., sports as a kind of religion, muscular Christianity, evangelicalism in sports, ethical issues related to gender, race, and the body, sportsmanship, etc.) in more depth. Some of the cases develop these themes directly. Others are based on a few specialized books about religion and sports, and some follow recent events and developments that are not likely to be part of the basic curriculum. Here there is an opportunity to use these cases as special projects. I also selected cases from a wide variety of religious traditions, geographic locations, and sports. I did this to provide a breadth that is usually lacking in courses on religion and sports that focus primarily on the United States and its "holy trinity" of football, baseball, and basketball. The cases are all drawn from real events and conflicts, not hypothetical situations. Some took place in the past, while some are still developing. Yet even the historical cases have contemporary relevance; for example, the proposed boycott of the 1936 Berlin Olympics by American Jewish athletes resonates with other efforts to boycott the Olympics, such as efforts by LGBT groups to boycott the 2014 Winter Olympics in Russia to demonstrate their distress at antigay legislation in that country. Each case concludes with suggested readings and possible activities for students. The activities build on one another, but can also be used separately. Each case also lends itself to further exploration, and the cases can become introductory materials for students to write their own research papers or do sustained projects for which examples and guidelines are provided.

The cases do not appear in any particular order, except for the last one. Depending on the course, the instructor can choose to use the cases to correspond to textbook chapters in another work, to follow an historical trajectory, to focus on topics related to different religions or sports, or to highlight issues in sports and society or popular culture. The concluding case, "What Would Phil Jackson Do?," provides an introduction to some of the issues facing sports figures today as well as the opportunity to synthesize learning in all the other cases.

I hope the book will also be useful in more general courses on religion in society, popular culture, ethics, sports in society, and sports history. Instructors in these courses might choose to use this text as the reading for a unit on religion and sport or choose one or two cases that might support the educational goals of the course. It is also possible this book could become a primary text for a course on religion, sports, and human difference because of its global focus and breadth of interests.

If you do find this text helpful in teaching (or have thoughts about how it might have been improved), I will welcome your feedback.

Philadelphia, Pennsylvania
ralpert@temple.edu

ACKNOWLEDGMENTS

I am grateful to have colleagues in the academic world who share my enthusiasm about sports and religion. Terry Rey, Eleanor Myers, Julie Byrne, and Amanullah De Sondy read portions of this manuscript and were enormously generous with their time and suggestions on how to make this a better book; I hope I followed them well. I am even more grateful to my other colleagues Lori Ginzberg, Avi Alpert, Pamela Barnett, and Marcus Bingenheimer who read portions and sent me in helpful directions despite their lack of enthusiasm about the subject matter. The anonymous readers also provided excellent feedback, and I am in their debt. I am also deeply appreciative of the efforts of Scott Singer, who read this manuscript while studying for his comprehensive examinations in religion and sport, offered helpful suggestions, and was kind enough to say it helped him in his preparation for exams. (He passed with flying colors, by the way.)

When I open a book, I go straight to the photographs. But I would never claim to have a discerning eye, so help in this department was crucial. I am most grateful to Tricia Gesner of AP Images and the staffs of the John F. Kennedy Library and the Cathedral of St. John the Divine; to photographers Seal Pla, Ross Watson, and Oliver Becker; and to collectors Josh Miller and Joel Wagner for making the process of gathering photos so pleasant. The most important person in this process was my daughter Lynn Alpert, who knows (and does) photography better than she will ever admit. She deserves all the credit for editing the images for this book.

Wendy Lochner, my editor at Columbia University Press, conceived this project and encouraged me to dream about it. Press staff members Christine Dunbar and Susan Pensak made this process work smoothly every step of the way.

I am grateful to Temple University for providing a Summer Research Grant. My colleagues in the Department of Religion and the Teaching and Learning Center at Temple and the Religion, Sport, and Play Group at the American Academy of Religion have provided intellectual companionship and camaraderie; I can't think of better places to think about teaching, religion, and sports.

Finally, thank you Christie for putting up with me and my love for sports, which at the end of the day can't hold a candle to my love for you.

RELIGION AND SPORTS

Introduction

WHY STUDY RELIGION AND SPORTS, ANYWAY?

Fig. 0.1. The Sports Bay Window at the Cathedral of St. John the Divine, New York City. Courtesy of the Church of the Cathedral of St. John the Divine, New York City.

On June 4, 2013, a baseball game between the Philadelphia Phillies and Miami Marlins went into extra innings. John Mayberry Jr., one of my favorite players, an outfielder for the Phillies who majored in political science when he played college baseball at Stanford University but has never quite realized his potential in the majors, and who had only been inserted into the game as a defensive replacement in the seventh inning, hit a solo home run to tie the game in the bottom of the tenth and a grand slam walk-off home run to win it in the bottom of the eleventh. As his teammates greeted him at home plate, doused him with Gatorade and covered his face with a shaving cream "pie," the radio announcers proclaimed him the first player in baseball history to have two extra inning home runs, one of which was a walk-off grand slam. It was a high point in an otherwise dismal season for my hometown team. My daughter, who was at the game, texted "walk-off grand slam?!?!?!?!" as I sat up in bed, roused out of my sleep, with tears in my eyes and a profound feeling of joy and well-being that would, by some, be labeled religious.

In its early years of development beginning in the 1970s, the field of study known as religion and sports (or *sport* in Great Britain and in most scholarship about this topic) could have been summarized in a nutshell in the anecdote I have just described. Scholars of religion and kinesiology (most notably Michael Novak, Shirl Hoffman, Charles Prebish, Andrew Cooper, and Joseph Price) analyzed the ways sports resembled religion. Some went so far as to define sports as a new form of religion. Collectively, they and others provided ample anecdotal evidence to support their theories, for which my experience is simply additional confirmation. Elements such as the special language (my description contains phrases as incomprehensible to the uninitiated as one finds in any religious tradition), the fallible hero who makes good, the ritual celebrations, the connection to a historic tradition, the meticulous keeping of records, the loyalty of fans across generations, and the sense of a cosmic connection to something outside oneself—all are markers of religious experience as it is commonly understood.

A fine and compelling beginning to the conversation, but if that were the only connection between religion and sports it would not be a field of study worthy of your attention unless, of course, you were a practitioner; someone like myself whose personal experience made you a believer in the religion of sports in one of its many manifestations. (I confess to being ambireligious; I could have described a similar powerful experience as a basketball fan, watching the Olympics or the World Cup, or, in my youth, playing volleyball.) But there's more to the story of the interrelationship between religion and sports that makes its telling, and the opportunity to study it, worthwhile not only for insiders but for anyone who wants to gain a deeper understanding of how these critical cultural practices contribute to our world today.

Sports and religion are two central facets of contemporary life that are deeply rooted in cultures around the globe. Both spheres can be enriching and ennobling influences, and both can be the locus for social evils—greed, corruption, commercialism, racism, sexism, homophobia, xenophobia. Studying the interconnections between sports and religion gives us an opportunity to understand how these key aspects of society influence our political and cultural lives and provide ways to understand human experience and its meaning and purpose. Sports have been studied primarily from the perspectives of ethics, law, sociology, psychology, economics, and the various dimensions of human difference (most notably race and gender). Adding religion to the conversation underscores the importance of sports as one of the most popular and significant dimensions of human experience.

In this introduction I will explore different ways religion and sports have been defined and how those definitions determine our understanding of their connections and conflicts. We will look at how religions have devalued sports or made peace with it and even used sports to gain adherents. We will look at how religions have incorporated sports and physical activity into their institutions, values, beliefs, and practices. We will also seek to understand how sports and individual athletes employ religious beliefs and practices to meet their personal goals. We will examine what happens when sports and religion come into conflict over questions of ethics and power. Separately, and together, religion and sports provide meaning and sustenance to many. Understanding their contributions to our lives will help make more sense of the world in which we live and improve our ability to communicate across cultural differences.

To gain maximum benefit from the study of religion and sports, it will be important to grapple with questions raised by this field of study that affect how we live today. After introducing the questions raised by examining the relationship between religion and sports, we will apply that learning by looking at case studies based on actual events to test this theoretical knowledge in real-life situations. The case studies present dilemmas created by the intersection of religion and sports: whether sports itself can really be viewed as a religion, whether religion and sports are compatible, what happens when religious beliefs and practices come into conflict with sports, and whether religions have an obligation to speak out about the ethical issues in sports today. Examining actual cases will connect classroom learning to real life, develop new perspectives on religion and sports, and provide a chance to respond to the challenges and conflicts in this arena. Reading about these cases, examining the views of experts and the people involved, will provide opportunities for staking out a position on these issues.

DEFINING RELIGION

Of course, when we talk about religion we think we know what we mean. But scholars in recent years have questioned the term itself. What is *religion?* It may come as a surprise, but there's a lot of disagreement about what the word actually means.

From the perspective of etymology, it's a puzzling word, even from the start, as we don't really know its linguistic origin. It is often suggested that the word comes from the Latin *religare,* "to tie or bind back." But, even if that's the source of the term (and there's no general agreement that it is), it doesn't tell us much. We do know that before the modern era religion in the West was equated with "Christian truth" and to be religious meant simply to believe in the Christian God.

Whatever the word meant originally, it came into formal usage as European scholars beginning in the eighteenth century sought to understand the relationship between their culture and others around the globe. It was their goal to make connections across time and space to determine what all cultures have in common. They also were coming to the realization that human beings, not a divine power, had created a variety of religious systems. They came to see Christianity as one belief system among many around the world as they met practitioners of what they labeled Hinduism, Buddhism, and "primitive religion" whose practitioners didn't necessarily have a name for their own beliefs and practices, and they wanted to understand how their own belief system compared to others. In this way, "world religions" became an object of study in Christian Europe and later North America. (If you're interested in this idea, take a look at Tomoko Masuzawa's *The Invention of World Religions*.)

Initially scholars assumed that the common thread among religions was that they all shared a belief in a god or gods. Others began to question this proposition (especially as they examined non-European cultures like those in China and realized most Buddhists, for example, did not believe in a god or gods or even practice one single religion; most people in China combine elements of Confucian, Daoist, and Buddhist beliefs and practices in their own lives) and modify that definition. Religion thus came to be understood as what humans believed about the existence of a transcendent force outside themselves that they perceived as powerful and other: described by Rudolph Otto as the holy. While this definition still focused on the supernatural, some scholars suggested the essence of religion might be simply what a person does in solitude (A. N. Whitehead) or what was someone's "ultimate concern" (Paul Tillich). But these definitions had something in common—the quest for one essential element that all religions shared. Many people and most dictionaries continue to define religion as the worship of a deity. We shall see that someone who views religion from this perspective is likely to be perplexed about (or even vexed by) comparing religion to sports.

For scholars of religion that definition was limited and limiting. While it may capture an essential feature of what we mean when we say religion and make religion simple to understand, it doesn't get at the deeper issues that are part of a religious worldview. Later scholars, primarily sociologists and anthropologists, became less interested in defining what religion *is* (its essence), and more curious about what religion *does*, or its function.

These scholars broadened the definition of religion to see it as a system that included not only what people believed but what they did about it (ritual practices like prayer, text study, and the creation of objects of veneration), what kind of laws, ethics, and values they derived from it, and what kind of institutions they built in order to organize their lives around it. The standard functionalist definition of religion was coined by Emile Durkheim in 1912: "a unified system of beliefs and practices relative to sacred things, that is to say, things set apart and forbidden—beliefs and practices which unite into one single moral community called a Church, all those who adhere to them." So a typical functionalist definition of religion might more simply be something like what I learned from my own college professor, Theodor Gaster, who taught that "religion is a system of beliefs and practices whereby groups of human beings attempt to regulate their role in the scheme of things." Or it might be reduced even further to what I call the 3Bs: behaving, believing, and belonging. Or it might be more complex, as described by anthropologist Clifford Geertz : "a system of symbols which acts to establish powerful, pervasive, and long-lasting moods and motivations in men by formulating conceptions of a general order of existence and clothing these conceptions with such an aura of factuality that the moods and motivations seem uniquely realistic." (Let us assume that if Geertz were writing today he would have said humans rather than men.) Psychologists, too, like William James began to study how religion functioned in the individual's psyche and what role it played in determining how humans understand their place in the world. How individuals perceive and define religious experience is also an important aspect of defining religion, and a highly subjective one.

While definitions of religion based on essence were often thought to be too narrow, functionalist definitions were often criticized for being too broad. If we really were defining religion based on what purpose it served in societies, didn't many phenomena (such as patriotism, political systems, and sports) also function in the same way? Obviously, functional definitions would be quite useful for people who understood sports as their religion and for those who want to use the category to mean a particular variation of a "worldview" or "culture" primarily focused on how groups of people negotiate making meaning in their lives. One such definition by David Chidester stands out; to him religion is "a way of being a human person in a human place." And both essentialist and functional definitions tended to make claims of universality—all religions at all times could be contained within the definition.

In recent times, scholars of religion have moved beyond looking for a definition that would be all-encompassing. Some argue that seeking out a definition is a futile enterprise with unsatisfying results, and the concept of "world religions" is a useful tool only for the purposes of comparative academic study. Others settle on understanding religion through the lens of what philosopher Ludwig Wittgenstein called "family resemblance." His idea suggests that, like "cousins," world religions are alike in that they bear some, but not all, characteristics in common and emphasize different dimensions depending on their different values. The systems we today call world religions (Islam, Christianity, Judaism, Buddhism, Hinduism, Daoism, Confucianism, African Traditional Religions, various new religious movements, Sikhism, Shinto, and the list goes on) sit somewhere on a continuum in regard to expressions of the following dimensions as delineated by religion scholar Ninian Smart: ritual, narrative and mythic, experiential and emotional, social and institutional, ethical and legal, doctrinal and philosophical, and material. Some religions may focus more on rituals (Santeria, for example) while others are more based on narrative (Hinduism or Judaism) or doctrine (Bah'ai comes to mind here). Smart's tool is useful for mapping religions and understanding them as living, breathing, changing phenomena that may share characteristics but use and express them quite differently.

Most people who look at religions that way are also inclined to remind us that no one religion is itself monolithic, and differences within a given religion may be even greater than the differences between religions. So, using the family analogy, groups we call Christian—Baptists, Quakers, Mormons, and Catholics, for example—are also more like "cousins" than siblings, and Unitarians and humanist Jews may have more in common with each other than they do with their more traditional coreligionists.

If we accept the utility of the category "religion," Smart's tool is helpful. Mapping religions in this way reminds us both of their similarities and differences and keeps us from allowing religion to become so vague as to be meaningless or so narrow as to exclude phenomena that might well be studied comparatively.

But we should also remember that religion does not stand apart from other aspects of society. Rather, religion should also be understood as moving across national boundaries ("crossing," as Tom Tweed would suggest) and being intertwined with politics, economics, and aspects of popular culture, like sports.

DEFINING SPORTS

Defining sport(s) is also a challenge. The dictionary definition is simple—a physical activity governed by rules and involving competition. But scholars of sports make the definition more specific, distinguishing modern sports from its ancient roots in play and leisure activity. Physical activity in sports incorporates a formally learned craft that requires physical exertion and the use of complex skills. These physical activities are not only governed by rules, but those rules are generally standardized, enforced through an institutional framework, and formally adjudicated. Sports, as institutions of public culture, have a history that includes record keeping and other particular traditions. Sports scholars remind us that sports is rooted in playing games, as was defined by Johan Huizinga, that are pleasure-based, informal recreational activities, and sports provides similar personal satisfaction for its participants. But its formal and competitive nature opens the possibility for external reward, often derived from the final dimension of sports that is predicated on its public aspect: the business of creating spectacle and the opportunity for (paid) spectatorship.

Using this particular definition of sports eliminates recreational activities like children's playground games and walking, as well as competitive activities that are not primarily physical but mental (chess or poker), motorized (boat or car racing), or electronic (video gaming). Defining sports in this narrow frame also reinforces cultural values (competition over cooperation, work over leisure) and privileges sports participants who have resources and social supports for their activities (men, people with wealth, and the able-bodied). For these reasons some scholars like David Andrews define sports more simply and expansively as varied expressions of physical culture. Or, like Stanley Eitzen, they divide sports into the categories of informal, organized, collegiate, and corporate. Or, like Jay Coakley, they refuse to define sports, preferring to ask questions about why certain values and activities are supported above others rather than accepting the status quo.

We might also introduce Smart's tool for mapping religions into this conversation. Like religions, the variety of phenomena we know as sports could be seen as "cousins" that share many, if not all, the characteristics we have delineated: playing games, competition, rules, institutionalization, physical skills, spectacle and spectatorship, personal and external reward, formal learning, and historical traditions. These characteristics help us understand what we mean when we talk about sports but permit us to think about sports in more creative and inclusive ways.

Clearly religion and sports are distinct realms of society. But the worlds of religion and sports connect to each other in interesting and surprising ways. In the rest of this essay I will introduce four different ways that religion and sports interconnect: Part 1 takes up the idea that sports are a religion. Part 2 looks at the place religion has in sports and that sports plays in religion. In part 3 we examine what happens when conflicts arise between religion and sports. Part 4 elucidates some of the ethical dilemmas that arise in the world of sports and opens the question of how religion might contribute to resolving them. Each of these issues will be illustrated by the case studies that follow.

PART 1: WHY DO PEOPLE THINK SPORTS ARE A RELIGION?

Looking at the criteria that constitute religion and sports in their respective sets of "family resemblances," there would appear to be little overlap. But while religion has never been thought to be a sport, many have written eloquently about their perception (and experience) of sports as a religion. If we are going to consider sports as religion, we must begin with accepting the premise that religion is a broad category that is not limited to the standard list of "world religions." This frame of reference begins with the notion of civil or cultural religion that dates back to the writings of the philosopher Jean-Jacques Rousseau in 1762. Rousseau described the ways the state uses features normally associated with religion (symbols, rituals, beliefs) to create a social contract among its citizens. Rousseau was writing in the era when Christianity was being replaced by secularism as the foundation of the nation-state and people in Europe were becoming aware of the existence of other religious systems. Durkheim, the sociologist who originated the functional way of looking at religion, developed the concept of civil religion further, identifying elements of public life as "sacred."

In the mid-twentieth century, American sociologist Robert Bellah provided a full blueprint for civil religion, using American political and public life as his example. He described how the country shaped its history (the American Revolution as sacred beginning), values (freedom and liberty), holiday celebrations (July Fourth as the sacred birthday of the nation), symbols (the Washington monument as tribute to the "father" of the country, the American flag as object of veneration), heroes (Washington, Jefferson, Franklin), and sacred texts (the Declaration of Independence and Constitution) into a full-fledged set of beliefs, rituals, and institutions that provided a sense of meaning, which together constitute the American civil religion.

In this schema, religion is associated with elements of culture such as symbols and rituals, beliefs, and institutions. It is important because of what it does (provide meaning) rather than what might form its essence (the worship of a particular deity or deities). Therefore any cultural phenomenon that provides a powerful mechanism for making meaning could be understood to function as a religion. This theoretical structure is further explored by religion scholar David Chidester in the realm of popular culture. Chidester uses the example of "the church of baseball" to explain the workings of phenomena of popular culture like politics, sports, and music as contemporary sites for meaning making.

Monotheistic religions that require adherents to maintain allegiance to only one religion (as I have already suggested, this doesn't hold true for some Asian or indigenous religions) seem to have no problem making room for their followers to participate in civil and popular religions as well. Given the power of sports in many cultures around the world to frame meaning through symbols, rituals, institutions, and beliefs, the notion of sports as a version of civil religion makes eminent sense. But many scholars have gone beyond this suggestion, using this framing to claim stronger connections between religion and sports.

Sociologist Harry Edwards was among the first to compare religion and sports, making a list of thirteen similarities between them. Edwards included elements like saints, ruling patriarchs, high councils, scribes, symbols of faith, and seekers of the kingdom. His linguistic choices made it clear that he was using Christian categories, but the elements he described made an apt comparison. Over the years other analysts of sports and religion have provided descriptions and examples that amplify Edwards's list and fit well into the elements of religion as delineated by Ninian Smart.

Ritual

Sports certainly provides opportunities to create significant ritual experiences. Sports heroes become sanctified figures, the subject of hagiographic biographies, immortalized in statues and halls of fame. Sports figures who sin (through violating sporting rules or general bad behavior) become object lessons and fallen figures. Followers participate in pilgrimages to holy sites (from *stadia*—remember *Field of Dreams?*—to halls of fame). The sports calendar (as described by Joseph Price in *From Season to Season*) marks the variety of holy events (golf and tennis tournaments, baseball's World Series, the Olympics, the World Cup, the Super Bowl) and the rhythm of the year for each individual sport. Further, athletes and fans develop gestures and acts that comprise rituals of celebration (from end zone dances to songs and chants) to mark their hopes and as expressions of gratitude. Sports also include, famously, superstitions (often associated with gestures, clothing, and equipment) that take on a ritual nature.

Narrative and mythic expression

Sports have histories that are narrated by scribes and kept in record books. The legends and stories of great exploits and tragedies are kept in written (and now digital) compendia, described and analyzed by sports commentators and announcers, recorded and preserved on visual media, and passed down across generations as part of mythic lore and tradition. Legends of famous events (Jesse Owens's four Olympic gold medals, Babe Ruth's sixty home runs) are required knowledge for participants and fans.

Experiential and emotional

Sports provides a location for the expression of a range of emotions including awe, gratitude, devotion, joy, sin, regret, grief, and loss. Sports researchers, most notably Mihaly Csikszentmihalyi, have documented the experience of "flow," or being "in the zone," likened to a mystical connection where athletes achieve a heightened state of awareness that opens a window to the transcendent, providing a glimpse of ultimate reality.

Social and institutional

Sports are organized into teams that represent cities, countries, or other institutions, from religious to commercial. They foster competition and also set social boundaries that differentiate groups from one another. These teams are also hierarchically structured into leagues that are run by those in charge of determining the rules of play and making business arrangements. Like more traditional religions, they tend toward patriarchal dominance and, like some religions, are gender segregated. The communities that develop around teams provide a social structure and network for followers not unlike those provided by houses of worship and denominational organizations.

Ethical and legal

Sports are bound by rules of play and organized according to codes of behavior. Sports figures, like clergy, are expected to behave in exemplary ways and held up to public shame if they do not. Sports are often described as valuable because they inculcate values (discipline, fair play, teamwork) or criticized as places where competition, hazing, and overwork bring out the worst in participants.

Doctrinal and philosophical

Sports are codified in books of instructions and are the locus of projects of individual identity formation. They are the subject of philosophical analysis that probes their deeper meaning.

Material

Sports equipment, uniforms, and paraphernalia (baseball cards, programs, and trophies) are considered holy objects, collected and venerated.

Catholic theologian Michael Novak wrote the *Joy of Sports: End Zones, Bases, Baskets, Balls, and the Consecration of the American Spirit* in 1976. It is the classic work that suggests in lyrical language and through passionate argument that sports resemble traditional religions because they are based on similar structures and meet the same personal and social needs. Although he limits his examples to the "holy trinity" of American sports (baseball, basketball, and football), his theoretical framework can be applied more broadly. Novak's comparison is based on what he calls the seven seals: sacred space, sacred time, rooting, a bond of brothers (a eucharist-like community), agon (inspired struggle), competing, and self-discovery. Through these sporting elements humans are allowed transcendent moments, "glimpses of eternity."

Charles Prebish, a scholar of Asian religions, wrote *Religion and Sport: The Meeting of Sacred and Profane* in 1993. He was the first to describe sports not only as "religion-like" but to stake a claim for sport as a bona fide religion. After reviewing the similarities between sports and traditional religions, Prebish summarizes: "What it all boils down to is this: if sport can bring its advocates to an experience of the ultimate, and this . . . experience is expressed through a formal series of public and private rituals requiring a symbolic language and space deemed sacred by its worshippers, then it is both proper and necessary to call sport itself a religion. It is also reasonable to consider sport the newest and fastest-growing religion, far outdistancing whatever is in second place" (74).

Joseph Price's edited volume, *From Season to Season: Sports as American Religion,* focuses on how specific sports manifest religious expression. These authors claim an affinity with the constructions of civil religion, but also acknowledge a debt to scholar of religion Mircea Eliade who explained how phenomena from the secular realm could be understood as sacred if they are symbols that exhibit a potential for pointing toward the transcendent in the realms of time and space. Eliade labeled these manifestations hierophanies and suggested they were not restricted to organized religions, but could be found anywhere in the secular world. The essays illustrate particular moments during the (liturgical) calendar where sports manifest the sacred. More recently, scholars have added specific examples of how a sport works as a religion. Eric Bain-Selbo's *Game Day and God: Football, Faith, and Politics in the American South* demonstrated college football's power as a religion for fans in the American south, and John Sexton has staked a claim for *Baseball as a Road to God*, no different from other, more traditional paths. Both Bain-Selbo and Sexton credit Eliade for their ability to see the sacred in the realm the world defines as "profane." Michael Zogry has studied the Cherokee Indian game of Anetso and presented a persuasive argument to help us understand it as both game and ritual in its development from the eighteenth century until today.

But Robert Higgs has challenged this perspective. In *An Unholy Alliance: The Sacred and Modern Sports*, Higgs and coauthor Michael Braswell call all these claims "sports apologetics." Although they are sports fans and see sports as opportunities to experience pleasure and appreciate beauty, they want to separate sports and religion into different realms. Higgs holds fast to the idea that the catalogue of traditional world religions is sacrosanct and challenges the notion that sports fits the criteria on which they are defined, calling the sports as religion narrative a version of "semantic abuse." He dismisses the idea of civil religions and critiques the reliance on Eliade, preferring the definition provided by Eliade's teacher, Rudolph Otto, who connected religion to the holy, which is "wholly other" and sports cannot, in his estimation, aspire to.

Although Higgs makes an argument for separating the concepts, he ultimately concedes that sports probably are a form of religion, only the "bad" kind. The religion of sports neglects the aspects of religion that are based on justice and compassion and mirrors religions that emphasize values like "discipline, duty, righteousness, winning, and obedience." Higgs claims that these were virtues in certain ancient traditions of Christianity (and their "pagan" forbears) modeled on the image of the knight rather than the shepherd. Sports, for Higgs, may be a manifestation of an ancient religion that incorporated games as dramatic reenactments, built on violence, winning, territorialism of sacred space, and sacrifice—a religion that we do not want to emulate.

Allen Guttmann, author of *From Ritual to Record,* also questioned the connection between religion and modern sports, arguing that, although ancient sports were unequivocally ritualistic in nature, sports in modernity is pursued for its own sake, and any connection to the holy has been severed. "We do not run," he says, "in order that the earth be more fertile" (26).

Higgs's and Guttmann's criticisms of religion as sports are important, as they keep a critical eye on sports, which, like traditional religions, has strong potential for corruption as well as for good. The connections made between religion and sports today is not about their "essence" but about how they are understood through the interpretive strategies and profound beliefs of those who experience them. Jeffrey Scholes and Raphael Sassower's *Religion and Sports in American Culture* argue for the necessity of thinking about these two cultural worlds as continuous and intertwined.

We'll explore whether sports can actually "count" as religion when we look at a situation that makes a strong case: the world of high school football in Odessa, Texas that H. G. "Buzz" Bissinger described poignantly in his book *Friday Night Lights.* We will also examine the case of Oscar Pistorius, the South African Olympic (and Paralympic) track and field star whose use of technologically "enhanced" prosthetic devices has raised questions about what it means to be human and what is just and fair, questions that are usually answered in the realm of traditional religions but in this case were being asked in the realm of sports. When, a few years after his Olympic triumph, Oscar Pistorius inspirational role model became Oscar Pistorius, the man convicted of culpable homicide in the killing of his girlfriend, his fall from grace also raised important religious questions about athletic heroes as moral exemplars. This case thus raises the question not only of whether sports is a religion but also whether sports has replaced religion as the arena where we ask ultimate questions about the meaning of life.

PART 2: DOES RELIGION HAVE A PLACE IN SPORTS OR SPORTS IN RELIGION?

Whether we are convinced or not that sports is a religion, there is no doubt that religion (primarily in the form of ritual and myth) and sports were integral to one another in ancient societies in ways that are different from the role world religions play in sports today. Ancient sports were not only founded in ritual as it is sometimes assumed; they were also meant for spectacle, entertainment, military training, competition, social advancement, and relaxation. But sports in ancient Japan, China, Greece, and Native American cultures (Algonquin, Aztec, and Mayan) were also all associated with beliefs about the cosmos and related ritual practices.

SPORTS IN THE ANCIENT WORLD

The Mayan ball game (*tlachtli*) is widely accepted as a classic case of ritualized sports. It dates back one thousand years before the common era and lasted for about two thousand years. Ball courts were found adjacent to temple complexes across Mesoamerica, the best known and best preserved being the court at Chichen Itza, Mexico. Losing players were sacrificed to the gods. Remains of their skulls, ball game artifacts, and drawings of the contests were discovered by archaeologists and written about by European explorers. The game derived from Central American creation myths about sacrifice and the cycles of nature. The Mayan myth explains how the gods of sickness and death of the underworld were ultimately defeated in a ball game by the hero twins Hunter and Jaguar. The twins' birth was the result of an earlier ball game between the gods and the First Fathers (representing the sun and Venus) that was held because the gods had been annoyed at the noise from the Fathers' incessant ball playing. During that game, the First Fathers were defeated and decapitated, their heads hung in a dead tree that miraculously becomes fertile. Later, the again alive head of the father who represented the sun impregnated a passing earth goddess who in turn gave birth to the hero twins. In a rematch of the original game, the twins are victorious, and this event signals the continuation of the cycle of life for which human sacrifice is considered a necessary correlate. The ritual ball game was reenacted in temple compounds. It was played with a large, heavy stone ball. A team scored when the ball touched the ground of the other team's territory. A similar game existed among the Aztecs and also the Algonquin tribe in North America.

Ceremonial running to demarcate an area that symbolized the cosmos is thought to have been part of ancient Egyptian ritual as early as 2600 BCE. Pharaonic hunting (with bow and arrow in chariots) was also observed as ritual. There are wall paintings from the fifteenth century BCE of the pharaoh Tuthmosis III hitting a ball with a stick to honor the god Hathor and drive evil from the kingdom.

In some areas of ancient China, martial arts were connected with philosophical goals of harmony and balance, expressed through the principles of yin and yang (balancing "male" and "female" elements) and *qi* (the life force). Scholars believe a primitive form of tai chi was developed to encourage the harmonious blending of mind and body. Buddhist teachers (notably, Bodhidharma, c. 525 BCE) developed martial arts traditions to encourage mindfulness. Although competition was antithetical to the values of harmony in these parts of China, in other geographic areas competitive sports flourished and in some instances had ritual aspects. Archery developed as a form of ritual ceremony. It is believed that dragon boat racing in rural China began as a part of an agricultural festival to ensure fertility of crops and later developed into a competitive sport. Kite flying was another sport in China that had a religious dimension based on the iconography that was displayed on kites to ward off evil spirits.

In Japan, sumō wrestling is associated with ancient ritual practice. Japanese mythology tells the tale of Takemikazuchi, who defeated rival gods in wrestling, making the Japanese the rulers of Japan. Sumō may have its origins in Shinto and Buddhist agricultural festivals, but there is no clear evidence. By the eighth century of the common era, sumo wrestling took its place as part of court ritual that established the power of the emperor and has been used subsequently to solidify Japanese national identity. The popular Japanese game of kickball, *kemari*, probably also had origins in a religious practice and later evolved into a widely participatory sport. Temple archery and swordsmanship were spiritual practices that developed from military practices in medieval Japan. They have been thought to be associated with Zen Buddhism, although many scholars believe that these ancient connections were really invented traditions; connections made by modern Japanese rulers to improve the image of Japan in the eyes of the West. (This strategy is common throughout the world; think of the claim baseball was invented by Abner Doubleday, a civil war hero, in Cooperstown, New York to substantiate its American origins and provide a reason to locate the Baseball Hall of Fame in that rural town.)

In the ancient Hindu text the Rig Veda, chariot races were part of the quest for immortality. In the Upanishads, archery is a means to reach Brahman, ultimate reality. Wrestling in Northern India (*pahlawan*), the roots of which are believed to date back to the fifth century before the common era, is a life discipline, taught by a guru and associated with the yoga traditions of Hindu religion, as explained by Joseph Alter.

Because of the modern Olympics, we are most familiar with the religious dimensions of ancient Greek games. Four sporting festivals, beginning seven hundred years before the common era, were held in honor of the Greek gods. The festival on Olympus honored Zeus; the Pythian festival at Delphi and the Nemean festival honored Apollo, and the Isthmian festival Poseidon. Athletic events (foot races, chariot races, discus, javelin throws, wrestling, and boxing) were held to propitiate the gods at sacred times in sacred places amidst extensive religious ceremony. In Ancient Rome, sports had no association with religion or ritual practice, but rather came to be connected to politics and the military and were disdained (especially the gladiatorial spectacles) by Christians for their brutality. The North African church father Tertullian was the most critical, arguing that participating in sports was antithetical to being a good Christian. When Christianity came to power, Roman sports fell into decline.

Although Paul used sports metaphors in his letters in the Christian Scriptures, it's not at all clear whether they were meant to harmonize with athletics or differentiate the Christian perspective from the Greek. In the

Hebrew Bible, physical strength was often mentioned in passing (Jacob, Samson, and David were all extolled for their prowess), but not highly valued. In the medieval era, Jews, Christians, and Muslims took part in ball games (primarily older versions of football, tennis, and bowling) especially during the spring season around Easter. Medieval Jews raised concerns about carrying tennis racquets on the Sabbath, which would violate prohibitions against work, but not about playing. Christians were encouraged to play on Sunday afternoons. Muslim and Jewish philosophers wrote about the importance of maintaining bodily strength since the body is a gift from God.

With the rise of Protestantism, Christian attitudes began to shift. Although Martin Luther was himself a bowler and saw virtue in recreational sports, John Calvin disdained sports, which he associated with gambling, idleness, and sensual pleasure, all things Calvin viewed as inimical to Christian living. The Puritans, who were Calvin's disciples, denounced games and sports in Europe and its colonies in North America. By the mid-seventeenth century, they outlawed contests on the Sabbath. They were joined in their antipathy by the Quakers and later by evangelicals, although attitudes toward sports and recreation were by no means monolithic among Protestants. Even Calvinists recognized the need to use recreation to refresh oneself to return to one's labors. Yet the dominant attitude prevailed, and after the American Revolution the "Protestant work ethic" took hold and sports were considered a detriment to building a prosperous society. You can find more detailed information about sports before the modern era in Allen Guttmann's *From Ritual to Record*, Nigel Crowther's *Sports in Ancient Times,* and the *Berkshire Encyclopedia of World Sport*.

MODERN SPORTS

But in the mid-nineteenth century in the United States and England the popularity of sports grew in spite of Protestant antipathy. While the wealthy had pursued gentlemanly sports (polo, hunting, golf, tennis, horse racing) in private clubs and the poor had been spectators and participants in rowdier sports (boxing and wrestling), industrialization and urbanization led to an increase in leisure time and a rising middle-class engagement in organized sports like baseball. Combined with the promotion of sports as amusement and as an avenue to values like team work and fair play, and new medical rhetoric about the benefits of a "sound body," the sporting life won many converts. Businesses, fraternal organizations, and social clubs organized teams to make sure their employees and members got exercise and made productive use of their newfound leisure time. Rather than continue to struggle against this increasingly important aspect of life, Protestants developed what came to be known as muscular Christianity.

Muscular Christianity developed first in England. It was popularized in Thomas Hughes's 1857 didactic novel *Tom Brown's Schooldays*, which celebrated the idea that manliness and sports were crucial to the development of boys into moral Christian men. Although sports traditions (gymnastics and blood sports like hunting and fencing) in continental Europe were more connected to militaristic than moralistic aims, liberal "Social Gospel" Protestant congregations in the U.S. northeast took the message of muscular Christianity to heart and built on the concept that sports developed Christian virtues of obedience, discipline, loyalty, cooperation, self-sacrifice, and endurance, which were becoming popular in Britain. Churches began to build gymnasia and sponsor their own teams. The magnificent Cathedral of St. John the Divine in New York commissioned a set of stained glass windows of figures in poses from various sports, depicted in the photograph at the beginning of this introduction. Social gospel–minded Christians also worked politically for urban reform to include parks and playgrounds for the poor and immigrant populations as they saw the opportunity to use sports to inculcate American values in those populations. Immigrants to the United States, mostly Catholic and Jewish, saw sports as an avenue of assimilation.

Sports and recreation flourished in Protestant circles as the international Young Men's Christian Association (YMCA) began a program aimed at keeping youth from being tempted by the evils of city life, encouraging them to maintain their Christian values of good sportsmanship through healthy activities provided in their gymnasiums and swimming pools. Although the Young Women's Christian Association was also developed, muscular Christianity in its inception had a decidedly masculinist perspective. Part of the reason for developing muscular Christianity was the perceived feminization of the religion, understood to be a weakening of its values and power. Although women were included in the new sports, their accomplishments and interests took a backseat to those of men, and modern sports developed, like most other institutions, a decidedly patriarchal orientation.

The YMCA movement was widely responsible for spreading the doctrine of muscular Christianity around the world. It was in under the influence of the YMCA culture that Canadian James Naismith invented the game of basketball in 1891 as a wholesome game to be played indoors. The woman's version was devised by Jewish immigrant Senda Berenson in the context of intercollegiate athletics a few years later, and in 1895 William Morgan invented volleyball as part of the mission of the YMCA to devise a less strenuous sport for older adults.

In this spirit, French baron Pierre de Coubertin created a modern version of the ancient Olympics, with the first modern summer games held in Athens in 1896. Coubertin's vision was to bring together nations in peaceful competition, which he hoped could avert war and develop international friendship and harmony that some saw as a secular religion. His Jesuit upbringing, meetings with British leaders of muscular Christianity, and reading *Tom Brown's Schooldays* deeply influenced Coubertin's vision of the moral potential of sports.

Conservative evangelicals did not absorb the passion to connect sports to Christian values until after World War II, but when they did so they created a new version of muscular Christianity that took hold deeply in their circles and continues today. Prior evangelical models of sportsmen who upheld Christian values in the early twentieth century were Billy Sunday, popular professional baseball player in the 1890s who left baseball to gain fame as an itinerant evangelical preacher and divorced the debased culture of sports from the moral Christian life, and Alonzo Stagg, a pioneering football coach who in contrast connected his Christian faith to his sporting values.

Renowned evangelical preacher Billy Graham is credited with creating interest in muscular Christianity in the era after World War II.

Graham, understanding the ascendancy of sports in American culture, invited sports figures (including the champion runner Gil Dodds) to give testimony at his revivals and used the metaphors of sports to describe the "race for Christ" in venues like Madison Square Garden and Yankee Stadium. Graham was America's most popular preacher throughout the 1950s, and his association with muscular Christianity was a key part of his success. His organization, Youth for Christ, was another vehicle through which sports and Christian living connected.

The 1950s also saw the development of a new version of muscular Christianity, which Frank Deford named Sportianity. This was an effort to evangelize athletes themselves and then use them as instruments to promote Christian faith. These efforts were institutionalized through the development of organizations for Christian athletes as vehicles to strengthen their belief and incorporate prayer into the world of sports. As part of their missionizing efforts, Sports Ambassadors, founded in 1952, took the message of muscular Christianity to Asia. This group used sporting events as venues for revival meetings. The Fellowship of Christian Athletes was founded in 1954, and Athletes in Action (part of Campus Crusade for Christ) in 1956. These two organizations focused their evangelizing work on high school and college athletes and coaches, encouraging athletes to convert to Christianity and to demonstrate their commitments through success on the playing field, prayers in the locker room, and moral behavior on and off the field. In 1973, Baseball Commissioner Bowie Kuhn approved the creation of Baseball Chapel, which to this day provides prayer services before games at almost every baseball park in the U.S. and many in Latin America.

By the 1970s, sports chaplains became associated with virtually every collegiate and professional team in most sports. These chaplains provide religious services, Bible study sessions, and pastoral counseling. In the 1990s an evangelical Protestant group for men, the Promise Keepers, was founded by a former college football coach, Bill McCartney. Although its main concern was strengthening Christian men's devotion to family, their leaders engaged sports through use of rhetoric and metaphor and frequently used sports stadia as sites for their meetings. These organizations, along with various other Christian sports associations affiliated with specific sports (NASCAR and mixed martial arts prominent among them), are still thriving today. They are often criticized for accepting the values of sports culture (competition, heroism, self-control, traditional family values) rather than challenging them from a Christian perspective. You can read about the history of muscular Christianity and examine new efforts to develop a more critical Protestant theology of sports in books by Nick Watson and Andrew Parker, Tony Ladd and James Mathisen, Donald Deardorff II and John White, Clifford Putney, William Baker, Lincoln Harvey, Annie Blazer, and Craig Forney.

Although Protestant groups are the most prominent in their association of religion and sports in the United States, Catholics, Mormons, Jews, and Muslims have all made similar connections. You can read about many of them in *With God on Their Side: Sport in Service of Religion*. Catholic universities (most notably Notre Dame) developed a religious sports culture made famous by star athlete and Coach Knute Rockne in the early twentieth century. Most Catholic schools have clergy attached to their sports teams. The Catholic Youth Organization (CYO), founded in the 1930s, created a Catholic sports culture not unlike the YMCA programs. Catholic theologians, primarily in Europe, have, like their Protestant counterparts, begun to develop a theology of sports. You can find their writings in works by Kevin Lixey and the Pontifical Council for the Laity.

Mormons also valued physical fitness and sports, and sports flourished in their schools and communities. They attributed their success in sports like baseball and basketball in the early twentieth century to Mormon values that emphasized healthy living. See the article on "Muscular Mormonism" for more information.

Jews developed a program of muscular Judaism in Europe in the early twentieth century. The plan to make Jewish men "normal" through the development of masculine efforts such as sports was the brainchild of German Zionist Max Nordau. Jews who immigrated to Palestine developed the Maccabiah Games to parallel the Olympic contests in the 1930s when Jews were not welcome in European contests. And American Jews used sports as an avenue of assimilation to U.S. culture, excelling in basketball and boxing. The YM and YWHA (the Young Men's and

Women's Hebrew Associations, later renamed Jewish Community Centers) emphasized sports as part of their program to encourage assimilation to a fully American Jewish life. You can learn more about Jews and sports in books by Steven Riess, Jeffrey Gurock, and Peter Levine.

Islamic culture generally has positive attitudes to sports; especially those that have fitness of the body as their goal. Equestrian sports, archery, swimming, and hunting were important to early Muslim cultures in the Middle East. The introduction of Western sports, however, was opposed by clerical leadership in various Muslim countries including Turkey, Indonesia, and Iran; although today they are widely accepted. Beginning in 1953, Muslim countries have held their own versions of the Olympics, the Arab games. Concerns about gender segregation led to the creation of Women's Islamic Games, sponsored by the Islamic Federation of Women's Sport, which last took place in 2005. In the 1960s many prominent African American athletes converted to Islam, publicly changing their names and refusing allegiance to the American flag and conscription into the military. Muhammad Ali and Kareem Abdul-Jabbar were perhaps the best known Muslims in America, changing American perceptions about Islam. Essays in Magdalinski and Benn and a chapter of Baker are key discussions of Islam and sports.

Sports and religion have a long history of mutual interplay from ancient times to the present. While what we have described here are the positive connections, we shall see from our case studies that not everyone agrees that these connections are of value either to sports or religion. Christian athletes make a valuable contribution encouraging Christian youth to a life of prayer and devotion, but should idolized figures like Tim Tebow be used to sell the gospel? Having events like the Maccabiah encourage Jewish athleticism, but is it all right for a British soccer team to field an exclusively Jewish team? And who is to decide who is a Jew? Sumō Wrestling is assumed to have deep roots in Shinto religion, but were these religious roots fabricated for a nationalist purpose? The Baseball Chapel may be a great boon to Christian athletes, but should umpires be forced to pray (or listen to prayers) when their dressing room is the only available site for their services? While it's important that Catholic schools have priests and nuns that accompany them and cheer for them, is it worthy of faith to pray for victory in basketball games? We will address these kinds of questions in part 2 as we examine cases where the world of sports and religion intertwine in order to determine whether limits should be set to these connections. When do they interfere with sports? When do they interfere with the religious liberty of others?

PART 3: WHAT HAPPENS WHEN RELIGION AND SPORTS COME INTO CONFLICT?

What we have examined so far are connections between religion and sports that are mutually reinforcing and positive. Sports can have a function similar to religion when they help people construct meaning in their lives or experience the transcendent. In the ancient world, religion and sports were often closely linked through ritual practices. And world religions have found ways to utilize sports in their missions, using the popularity of sports and athletes as avenues for conversion and examples of positive values. But combining religion and sports may also cause conflicts for religious groups and individuals.

RELIGIOUS VALUES IN CONFLICT WITH SPORTS

At different times and places religious groups have seen sports as antithetical to their value systems. Ancient Christians found Roman sport traditions too violent and lacking purpose. Although medieval Christianity made peace with sports, early Protestants (and especially Puritans) thought sports distracted human beings from their primary life goals of devotion to work and to God. And Evangelical Christians railed against muscular versions of Christianity for almost a century.

Sports have also been popular throughout Asian history, although the competitive nature of sports has often caused tension in religious traditions that were focused on creating balance and harmony like Daoism and Buddhism. The authenticity of the celebrated connection between Buddhist meditative practice and martial arts and archery has been questioned by scholars, and traditional Buddhism had a neutral (and in some cases negative) attitude toward endeavors of the body in general. Sporting traditions in India were always strong, but the tension between the imported British colonial sports and indigenous Indian traditional sports that were more deeply connected to Hindu traditions remains.

Jews were believed to be a people of the book and not a people of the body. Although exceptions can be pointed out (some biblical figures like David and Samson, some ancient rabbis participating in Greek and Roman sports, an acceptance of leisure activities like racquet sports in medieval Europe, philosophers expressing support for a "sound body/sound mind" perspective), for the most part Jewish culture was not sports oriented. One could even argue that the development of muscular Judaism, the Maccabiah and the YMHA, were efforts to make Judaism more sports friendly and to make Jews more acceptable in Islamic and Christian cultures where they lived.

Traditional Islamic culture has positive attitudes toward sports, but problems have arisen in modern times integrating Western sports culture into Muslim societies. Some Muslim countries initially resisted the incursion of Western sports like soccer and cricket. In other cases they refused to compete in international events that included Israel, and their antipathy also set the stage for violence at the 1972 Olympics in Munich with tensions about memorializing the dead Israeli athletes still simmering at the London games in 2012. Islamic values of gender segregation have also been a source of tension. Unwillingness to send women to the Olympics (and the development of separate and gender-segregated international games) has raised questions for the International Olympic Committee about allowing participation from countries with all-male teams. Today including Muslim women athletes in modest dress is still causing tension in some Olympic sports (like judo), although creating special garments for Muslim women athletes has become a priority so that they can compete successfully on the international stage.

TIME FOR SPORTS AND TIME FOR RELIGION

One of the major sources of friction between sports and religion in Judaism, Christianity and Islam has been when the times for religious observance conflict with sporting events. In the past, and in some circles even today, devout Christians have refused to play games on their holy days. Puritans passed "blue laws" prohibiting commerce on Sundays. For most of U.S. history selling tickets for sporting events was prohibited, as was the sale of alcohol. The laws were deemed constitutional based on a Supreme Court ruling in 1961 that defined them as having a secular, not a religious, purpose. Most of these laws were challenged or circumvented locally by liberal Protestant, secular, Jewish, and Seventh Day Adventist sports entrepreneurs and have since been repealed, but some prohibitions of sporting activities on Sunday mornings still exist in certain states in the U.S. and also in Europe. The month-long fast during Ramadan has also created conflicts for Muslim athletes.

The most famous case of a Christian athlete's refusal to compete on Sundays was immortalized in the film *Chariots of Fire,* the story of the British long-distance runner Eric Liddell. Well-known Christian baseball owner Branch Rickey (the man who broke baseball's color line) refused to attend his own team's games when they were played on Sundays. The New Zealand Olympic women's basketball team forfeited their game when it was played on the Sabbath in 2008 at the request of two of their Mormon players. Mormon schools, like Brigham Young University, still do not schedule games or practices on Sunday, and some Mormon athletes have refused professional sports careers because they won't play on the Sabbath.

The Jewish Sabbath (sundown to sundown Friday to Saturday) is a time devoted exclusively to religious practice. In the strictest circles, the evening and day are reserved for prayer, study, and family time. But even in more liberal circles where sporting activities are permitted on Saturday afternoon, traditional prohibitions against travel, using electricity, operating machinery, and carrying objects would make playing or even watching sports a challenge. The same prohibitions are in place during major Jewish holy days. In Christian cultures where Sunday sports were traditionally restricted as well, conflicts for Jews abound as Friday nights and Saturdays were the time for leisure for the majority of citizens. Famous stories of Jewish athletes walking rather than driving to boxing matches (Barney Ross), agonizing over playing on the Jewish New Year (baseball star Hank Greenberg), refusing to pitch on Yom

Kippur (Sandy Koufax) make up an important part of Jewish sports lore. But those famous athletes were not themselves religious. The stories of Orthodox Jewish athletes giving up athletic scholarships because the teams played on Saturdays (basketball player Tamir Goodman) or teams negotiating to have their schedules changed (Houston's Beren Academy Stars high school basketball team) or leagues creating their own tournaments to avoid scheduling problems (Red Sarachek Basketball League) are legion. The plot of a recent Hollywood film about an ultra-Orthodox yeshiva's baseball team (*Yankles*) hinges on rescheduling the final game from Saturday to a weekday.

PUBLIC DISPLAYS OF RELIGIOUS COMMITMENT IN SPORTS

Athletes committed to their religious practices often experience dilemmas when they seek to express their religious commitments through markings on their body and the clothes they wear. Tim Tebow was permitted to ink New Testament verses into his eye black in college, but the NCAA subsequently banned it because of concerns raised by fans that disliked the display of religion. All inscriptions on eye black had been prohibited by the National Football League for years prior to this, so Tebow was not allowed to bring messages from the gospel to the playing field when he turned professional. (His fans who objected to the ruling continued to bring signs with biblical citations to his games, however. John 3:16, his game day verse, was googled by more people than any other term during the playoffs that day.) Religious jewelry and tattoos have also been accepted in some circumstances and prohibited and criticized in others. For the most part, religious symbols have been sanctioned if they are safely secured and don't have the potential to cause bodily harm in the course of play.

For Muslims, Sikhs, and Orthodox Jews, clothing is an area of conflict playing sports. Muslim women, Sikh men, and Orthodox Jewish men and women are required by their respective traditions to cover their heads (for women their hair) at all times. Most sports accommodate Jewish men wearing a yarmulke (skull cap) to show respect for

God, provided it is held firmly in place, and Orthodox Jewish women who are permitted to wear wigs by their tradition generally have not had problems. Sikh men also cover their heads as a symbol of respect by wearing turbans. For many Sikh men, the turban holds in place their long hair, which they are forbidden to cut. While Sikh men usually are permitted to wear turbans even under other headgear, the Quebec Soccer Federation (QSF) banned turbans in what appeared to be an anti-immigrant gesture. The QSF was finally suspended because of this rule by the Canadian Soccer Association in 2013. The International Judo Federation bans headscarves. In the 2012 Olympics, a Saudi woman was allowed to compete, but only after special interventions. The International Basketball Federation came under criticism for banning Sikh turbans and Muslim hijab in the summer of 2014.

Many sports have accommodated traditional Muslim and married Jewish women's dress, which requires that no part of their bodies be exposed to public view. In some cases, rules about appropriate dress have been changed to make it possible for religious women to compete. Manufacturers have also been working on modest clothing that is suitable for swimming and other sports, and special hijabs have been created for sportswear. As we will discuss, none of these prohibitions on women's dress are necessary in gender-segregated spaces; the prohibition is against men seeing women's bodies. But gender segregation itself is another place where religion and sports collide.

PART 4: RELIGION AND ETHICAL DILEMMAS IN SPORTS

Modern sports were founded on the idea of the fostering of good values including healthy lifestyles, teamwork, sportsmanship, and equal opportunity in the form of a "level playing field." But in recent years "the great sports myth" has begun to crumble. We witness unfair treatment of athletes based on race, gender, sexual orientation, national origins, and ability (not to mention religion) and unethical treatment of animals. Many athletes use illegal and unhealthy means to gain a competitive edge. Teamwork takes a back seat when athletes seek only personal gain. Violence in sports has caused injuries (and death) to athletes and fans. Is there a place in sports for religious values?

GENDER, SEXUALITY, DISABILITY, RACE

Wojdan Ali Seraj Abdulrahim Shahrkhani was allowed to compete in the Judo matches in the 2012 Olympics because she was one of two women that Saudi Arabia allowed to represent her country. The International Olympic Committee and human rights groups made tireless efforts over the years to compel Saudi Arabia to send women to the Olympics. They were the last nation to relent. Sending two women (the other was a runner) for the first time averted a threatened ban on the country's future Olympic participation. In conservative sectors of Islam it is indecent for men to watch women play sports without proper modest attire, and Muslim countries have dealt with this problem by organizing separate quasi-Olympics for men (the Arab Games) and women (Islamic Countries' Women's Sports Solidarity Games). While there has been much disapproval of these gender-segregated events in Christian nations, sports itself is almost universally based on the principles of gender segregation; men and women do not compete against one another. Religiously affiliated leagues in other traditions have also had to consider the question of gender segregation in their own teams and tournaments. The question of gender segregation in sports is and will continue to be a subject of debate.

How gender segregated spaces like sports deal with the presence of transgender people, whose desires are often spiritual in nature, need to be considered. The question of why religions are criticized for gender segregation when it is a universally accepted dimension of sports culture deserves further discussion. Perhaps religions could have helpful perspectives to add in cases like deciding the fate of South African runner Caster Semenya, an athlete who sought to participate as a woman but who was subjected to heightened scrutiny and embarrassing testing because some raised suspicions that she wasn't sufficiently female.

Gay sexuality is also a contentious issue in the world of sports. While many women have publicly identified as lesbian athletes, gay men have not been comfortable being public about their sexual orientation. Religiously identified athletes have been at the forefront of mocking and censuring homosexuality. But not all religious institutions are homophobic, and many have worked against antigay attitudes in the religious world. Different groups have taken different approaches. There are dissenting organizations in more traditional religions like Mormonism, Islam, Catholicism, and Orthodox Judaism. Middle-of–the-road Protestant and Hindu groups continue to struggle over the issue. Liberal Protestant, Quaker, Jewish, and Buddhist groups strongly affirm gay rights and provide full inclusion.

But sports, particularly the "holy trinity" of football, basketball, and baseball, have been slower to welcome LGBT athletes in their midst. In 2013 the first active player in major U.S. sports, NBA center Jason Collins, publicly came out in a story in *Sports Illustrated*. Collins's racial background was incorporated into the story, but his religious commitment as a devout Christian received less attention. Early the following year Michael Sam, a defensive lineman at the University of Missouri, came out after his final college season but before the NFL draft. Drafted in a late round by the St. Louis Rams, Sam became the first openly gay man with the opportunity to play professional football. Although he didn't make the team, he accepted a position on the practice squad of the Dallas Cowboys and was greeted by protesting Christians when the season began. Sam's religious identity received little coverage, although his mother, a devout Jehovah's Witness, had as much concern about his playing football as his being gay. (Jehovah's Witnesses do not participate in organized sports.) Collins's and Sam's coming out stories will continue to play an important role in defining the relationship among sports, sexuality, religion, and race. It is likely that these events influenced Major League Baseball to hire Billy Bean, a former outfielder who came out after retirement, as their "Ambassador of Inclusion."

Sports are not only segregated by gender but also by physical ability. Athletes with disabilities (mental and physical) have, in recent years, been gaining visibility and opportunities to play in leagues and the Paralympics. But that segregation is being questioned. When Oscar Pistorius was allowed to run on prosthetic devices in the Olympics in 2012, questions arose about whether mainstreaming devalues Paralympic contests. Despite Pistorius's accomplishments, single amputee long jumper Markus Rehm was denied a place on the German national team in the European Athletics championship in 2014 for fear that his prosthetic device gave him an unfair advantage.

We have also seen more and more recent evidence that sports are where racism is expressed publicly. In 2014 the negative reactions to Seattle Seahawk cornerback Richard Sherman's provocative comments after the Super Bowl, the unenlightened thoughts about African Americans made by NBA Clippers owner Donald Sterling, and the unbridled antisemitism of Spanish soccer fans directed at Maccabi Tel Aviv all illustrated that our societies are not comfortable with racial diversity. Can religions play a role in changing the values that underlie this ignorant behavior?

RELIGIOUS PERSPECTIVES ON PERFORMANCE ENHANCEMENT

The case of Oscar Pistorius also raises questions about performance enhancement. His biomedically engineered prosthetic devices, known as "Flex-foot Cheetah" legs, were thought to give him an unfair advantage. Performance enhancements, whether devices like "cheetah legs," ingested chemical substances, and even the use of meditation, have come under scrutiny in sports circles. Is it ever ethical to use enhancements? What are the values that are called into question when athletes seek to gain advantage through performance enhancement techniques? Is perfection something to be desired? Does performance enhancement put health at risk? What does it mean for the nature of competition? Does it alter the rules of sports? These questions all have religious dimensions and should be something religious leaders and thinkers weigh in on. Yet the question has only recently begun to be addressed by scholars of religion and sports. Implementing religious values to enhance sports performance has its virtues, but should coaches be allowed to use religious methods like Zen meditation as part of their toolbox? Phil Jackson claimed that using Zen and Native American techniques was what made him a successful sports coach. But did Jackson's use of these techniques in basketball create an unfair advantage for his teams? Is meditation a performance enhancer, too?

RELIGIOUS PERSPECTIVES ON VIOLENCE IN SPORTS

Religions are often criticized for causing wars and encouraging violence in support of their beliefs. There is no doubt that religions have been the source of violence, wars, and strife. Violence is built into religious scripture—the bloody battles of Hindu gods, the intentional violence of Yahweh toward the nations in the Hebrew Bible, the crucifixion narrative and the Muslim holy wars (although we must be careful to note that holy war is only one meaning of the term *jihad*), and the widely held religious precept of sacrifice. And there are a variety of martial arts (forms of aikido, tai chi, and yoga) that are based on meditative practices, but also link spirituality and combat. Yet most religions claim that the pursuit of peace and harmony is their primary objective. In comparison, violence and brutality in sports is not criticized but accepted as part of the rules of the game. Sports have been understood as a safe arena that has replaced religion as a location for ritually enacted violence that provides a necessary catharsis for society, although some argue that the violence in sports gives permission for violence in society. Whereas Pierre de Coubertin's vision of sports as a peaceful way to channel competition has been successful in many respects, sports contests have also been a source of nationalistic pride and the site for international disputes. Unbridled patriotism has hurt sports and created an atmosphere of violence and tension. And gratuitous violence, like fights in hockey games, is viewed by some sports fans and owners as desired intensification of spectator interest. In recent years the cruelty to animals found in sports such as dogfighting, bullfighting, and cockfighting have come under closer scrutiny and protest. The deleterious effects of fan violence have also received more attention as the violence at soccer matches has increased in intensity and resulted in deaths. Another area of concern has been sports injuries, especially the concussions that are routine for soccer, football, hockey, baseball, and other contact sports played by children and adults. Yet religious leaders have been slow to speak out on these issues.

SPORTS AS A VENUE FOR RELIGIOUS PROTEST

At the same time, sports have been a place for religious groups to protest against national aspirations that have oppressed them. During the 1936 Berlin Olympics, some Jewish athletes protested Hitler's racial ideology by boycotting, while others protested by participating. They joined Jesse Owens, demonstrating their athletic skills.

The recent protests over the use of the name *Redskins* by the Washington professional football team showcases the role sports can play in assisting religious aspirations for freedom and equality. The use of Native American religious iconography by college and professional teams is still widespread, even though many teams changed their names when the matter was first protested in the 1980s. This situation demands that we ask, who "owns" these religious symbols, and what does their use convey?

SPORTSMANSHIP

Although sports and religion do have common values (fair play, teamwork, discipline), sports has also been the locus of cheating, ruthless competition, and individualistic, self-centered behavior. Sociologist Steven Overman sees these attributes as part of religion as well, in particular what he calls the "secular Protestant ethic." Do religious groups have an obligation to take responsibility for these attitudes and speak out against these practices?

Religion and sports have a long and complex association in virtually every time and place. For some people, playing and watching sports have provided an outlet for meaning making, ritual celebration, and connection to ultimate reality that functions for them like religion. Others are fascinated by the many different ways sports were part and parcel of ritual in the ancient world and have been used in service of traditional religions' aspirations in modern societies. And others have puzzled over some of the critical ethical questions of our times raised when religion and sports come into contact: violence, honoring human differences, social protest, and the quest for perfection.

The remainder of this book consists of case studies; stories that will illustrate questions raised in this introduction. The studies were deliberately chosen to reflect a variety of sports and religions and to expose how interactions between religion and sports have taken place in cultures around the globe. The case studies are designed to encourage further thought about what sports and religion mean for the human condition in our relationship to the environment, to other living creatures, and to each other. I hope you will keep an open mind as you read these cases, remaining curious rather than judgmental about phenomena and perspectives you haven't encountered before or find strange or peculiar at first glance. The ultimate goal is for you to find your place among those who have given serious thought to how religion and sports interconnect in society today and how both religion and sports provide meaningful ways for humans to find our place in the scheme of things.

RESOURCES

Alter, Joseph S. *The Wrestler's Body: Identity and Ideology in North India.* Berkeley: University of California Press, 1992.

Andrews, David L. *Sport-Commerce-Culture: Essays on Sport in Late Capitalist America.* New York: Peter Lang, 2006.

Bain-Selbo, Eric. *Game Day and God: Football, Faith, and Politics in the American South.* Macon, GA: Mercer University Press, 2009.

Baker, William J. *Playing with God: Religion and Modern Sport.* Cambridge: Harvard University Press, 2007.

Bellah, Robert. "Civil Religion in America." *Daedalus* 96.1 (January 1967): 1–21.

Benn Tansin, Gertrud Pfister, and H. A. Jawad. *Muslim Women and Sport.* London: Routledge, 2010.

Berkshire Encyclopedia of World Sport. Great Barrington, MA: Berkshire, 2005.

Blazer, Annie. *Playing for God: Sports Ministry, Gender, and Embodied Worship in Evangelical America.* New York: NYU Press, 2015.

Chidester, David. *Authentic Fakes: Religion and American Popular Culture.* Berkeley: University of California Press, 2005.

Coakley, Jay J. *Sport in Society: Issues and Controversies.* 11th ed. Boston: McGraw-Hill, 2014.

Cooper, Andrew. *Playing in the Zone: Exploring the Spiritual Dimensions of Sports.* Boston: Shambhala, 1998.

Crowther, Nigel B. *Sport in Ancient Times.* Westport, CT: Praeger, 2007.

Csikszentmihalyi, Mihaly. *Flow: The Psychology of Optimal Experience.* New York: Harper and Row, 1990.

Deardorff, Donald and John White, eds. *The Image of God in the Human Body: Essays on Christianity and Sports.* Lewiston, NY: Edwin Mellen, 2008.

Deford, Frank. "Religion and Sport." *Sports Illustrated* 44.16 (April 19, 1976): 88–102.

———. "The World According to Tom." *Sports Illustrated* 44.17 (April 26, 1976): 59–65.

———. "Reaching for the Stars." *Sports Illustrated* 44.18 (May 3, 1976): 44–60.

Durkheim, Émile. *The Elementary Forms of Religious Life.* Oxford: Oxford University Press, 2008.

Edwards, Harry. *Sociology of Sport.* Homewood, IL: Dorsey, 1973).

Eitzen, Stanley et al. *Sociology of American Sport.* Dubuque: Brown, 1978.

Eliade, Mircea. *The Sacred and the Profane: The Nature of Religion.* New York: Harcourt, Brace, 1959.

Forney, Craig A. *The Holy Trinity of American Sports: Civil Religion in Football, Baseball, and Basketball.* Macon, GA: Mercer University Press, 2007.

Geertz, Clifford. "Religion as a Cultural System." In *The Interpretation of Cultures: Selected Essays,* 87–125. New York: Basic Books, 1973.

Gurock, Jeffrey S. *Judaism's Encounter with American Sports.* Bloomington: Indiana University Press, 2005.

Guttmann, Allen. *From Ritual to Record: The Nature of Modern Sports.* New York: Columbia University Press, 2004.

Harvey, Lincoln. *A Brief Theology of Sport.* New York: Cascade, 2014.

Higgs, Robert J. *God in the Stadium: Sports and Religion in America.* Lexington, KY: University Press of Kentucky, 1995.

——— and Michael Braswell. *An Unholy Alliance: The Sacred and Modern Sports.* Macon, GA: Mercer University Press, 2004.

Hoffman, Shirl J. *Good Game: Christianity and the Culture of Sports.* Waco, TX: Baylor University Press, 2010.

———. *Sport and Religion.* Champaign, IL: Human Kinetics, 1992.

Hughes, Thomas and Arthur Hughes. *Tom Brown's Schooldays.* New York: Oxford University Press, 1989.

Huizinga, Johan. *Homo Ludens: A Study of the Play-Element in Culture.* Boston: Beacon, 1955.

James, William. *The Varieties of Religious Experience: A Study in Human Nature.* New York: Modern Library, 1936.

Kelly, Patrick. *Catholic Perspectives on Sports: From Medieval to Modern Times*. New York: Paulist Press, 2012.

Kimball, Richard. "Muscular Mormonism," *International Journal of the History of Sport* 25.5 (April 2008): 549–578.

———. "Sport and American Religion." In Steven Riess, ed., *A Companion to American Sport History*, 601–614. New York: Wiley-Blackwell, 2014.

Ladd, Tony and James A. Mathisen. *Muscular Christianity: Evangelical Protestants and the Development of American Sport*. Grand Rapids: Baker, 1999.

Levine, Peter. *Ellis Island to Ebbets Field: Sport and the American Jewish Experience*. New York: Oxford University Press, 1992.

Lixey, Kevin et al., eds. *Sport and Christianity: A Sign of the Times in the Light of Faith*. Washington, DC: Catholic University of America Press, 2012.

Magdalinski, Tara and Timothy John Lindsay Chandler, eds. *With God on Their Side: Sport in the Service of Religion*. New York: Routledge, 2002.

Masuzawa, Tomoko. *The Invention of World Religions; Or, How European Universalism Was Preserved in the Language of Pluralism*. Chicago: University of Chicago Press, 2005.

Novak, Michael. *The Joy of Sports: End Zones, Bases, Baskets, Balls, and the Consecration of the American Spirit*. New York: Basic Books, 1976.

Otto, Rudolf and John W. Harvey. *The Idea of the Holy: An Inquiry into the Non-Rational Factor in the Idea of the Divine and its Relation to the Rational*. New York: Oxford University Press, 1925.

Overman, Steven J. *The Protestant Ethic and the Spirit of Sport: How Calvinism and Capitalism Shaped America's Games*. Macon, GA: Mercer University Press, 2011.

Parry, S. J., Mark Nesti, and Nick Watson. *Theology, Ethics and Transcendence in Sports*. New York: Routledge, 2011.

Prebish, Charles S. *Religion and Sport: The Meeting of Sacred and Profane*. Westport, CT: Greenwood, 1993.

Price, Joseph L., ed. *From Season to Season: Sports as American Religion*. Macon, GA: Mercer University Press, 2001.

Pontifical Council for the Laity, ed. *The World of Sport Today: A Field of Christian Mission*. Vatican: Libreria Editrice Vaticana, 2006.

———. *Sport: An Educational and Pastoral Challenge*. Seminar of Study on the Theme of Sport Chaplains. Vatican: Libreria Editrice Vaticana, 2008.

Putney, Clifford. *Muscular Christianity: Manhood and Sports in Protestant America, 1880–1920*. Cambridge: Harvard University Press, 2003.

Riess, Steven A., ed. *Sports and the American Jew*. Syracuse: Syracuse University Press, 1998.

Rousseau, Jean-Jacques. *The Social Contract*. Baltimore: Penguin, 1968.

Scholes, Jeffrey and Raphael Sassower. *Religion and Sports in American Culture.* New York: Routledge, 2014.

Sexton, John Edward, Thomas Oliphant, and Peter J. Schwartz. *Baseball as a Road to God: Seeing Beyond the Game.* New York: Gotham, 2013.

Smart, Ninian. *Dimensions of the Sacred: An Anatomy of the World's Beliefs.* Berkeley: University of California Press, 1996.

Tillich, Paul and Robert C. Kimball. *Theology of Culture.* New York: Oxford University Press, 1959.

Tweed, Thomas. *Crossing and Dwelling: A Theory of Religion.* Cambridge: Harvard University Press, 2006.

Watson, Nick J. and Andrew Parker. *Sports and Christianity: Historical and Contemporary Perspectives.* New York: Routledge, 2013.

Whitehead, Alfred North. *Religion in the Making: Lowell Lectures, 1926.* New York: Macmillan, 1926.

Willis, Joe and Richard Wettan. "Religion and Sport in America: The Case for the Sports Bay in the Cathedral Church of Saint John the Divine," *Journal of Sport History* 4.2 (1977): 189–206.

Zogry, Michael J. *Anetso, the Cherokee Ball Game: At the Center of Ceremony and Identity.* Chapel Hill: University of North Carolina Press, 2010.

PART 1

WHY DO PEOPLE THINK SPORTS ARE A RELIGION?

In this section we will be examining two cases that help us understand why people have claimed that sports are their religions. What makes sports sacred to some people? Are sports symbols and rituals worthy of being identified as religious? Are they appropriate sites for people to invest with holiness? Do sports represent our highest values? Should sports heroes be idolized? Should they be held to a higher standard than other human beings? The high school football culture in Odessa, Texas is an example of what happens when sports becomes the "religion" of a municipality. In case 1, Buzz Bissinger's ethnographic account of life in Odessa, *Friday Night Lights,* we will highlight how sports can become a religion through the story of a small-town community that lives through their high school football team. Case 2, the story of double amputee runner Oscar Pistorius, will help us see how sports has raised questions understood to be religious about what it means to be human, how we understand justice and fairness, and what are the qualities a person needs to be a moral exemplar.

CASE 1
Friday Night Lights
HIGH SCHOOL FOOTBALL
AS RELIGION IN ODESSA, TEXAS

Fig. 1.1. Player reading a Bible in the locker room from *Friday Night Lights*. Robert Clark/INSTITUTE.

GOAL: Form a well-reasoned opinion about whether high school football should be understood as, is similar to, functions as, or is not at all a religion for the residents of Odessa, Texas.

READ: *Friday Night Lights: A Town, a Team, and a Dream* by H. G. Bissinger (Boston: Addison-Wesley, 1990).

H. G. "Buzz" Bissinger took a one-year leave of absence from his job as a reporter for a local newspaper, the *Philadelphia Inquirer,* to observe the experiences of a storied high school football team in Odessa, Texas, the Permian Panthers. Beginning in 1946, the Panthers were perennial contenders and had won several Texas state championships. Through the 1990s their Friday night games were the heart and soul of the town. From the beginning of the season until its end, the players, coaching staff, boosters, and cheerleaders (the Pepettes) spent all their time and energy preparing for, attending, and celebrating or mourning the results of the games. Odessa's weekly activities were centered on the team, and the town's attention focused on each game and each team member.

Bissinger was curious about the culture of high school football and wanted to understand how high school football defined life in Odessa. *Friday Night Lights* is a critically acclaimed journalistic account of Bissinger's experience chronicling the 1988 season in the context of the economic, racial, and social changes the town was experiencing. The book, which used the real names of the players and coaches, was made into a (fictionalized) major motion picture in 2004, and yet another version was adapted for television by the film's director, Peter Berg. The network series aired for five seasons (2006–2011). Although they did not garner a lot of popular attention, both the film and series were well received by critics. Bissinger's book continues to be widely read and used as a course text in college classrooms like this one.

Friday Night Lights highlighted racial, social, and economic issues in the oil-based boom or bust economy of this small town in West Texas, which had been cited by several magazine surveys in the 1980s as one of the worst places in America to live. But high school football was at the core of what made life livable, and the city made huge financial investments in the Panther team's stadium, equipment, and travel.

Bissinger was not himself interested in the question of whether high school football could be called a religion, and so this book provides a neutral platform for us to ask that question. For this case study, you must read *Friday Night Lights*. It is important to look at the activities associated with this case study BEFORE you read so that you can be on the lookout for the keywords, stories, descriptions, and quotations you will need to answer the questions. Although you will have no trouble accessing plot summaries and reviews on the Internet, and you might thoroughly enjoy the film and TV series, you will only be able to answer the questions posed here by reading the book.

ACTIVITIES

ACTIVITY 1

Part 1 at home

STEP 1

Review the section of the introduction to this text that provides a variety of definitions of religion and the section that lays out the arguments for and against understanding religion and sport.

STEP 2

Find five examples (quotations, stories, or descriptions) in *FNL* that illustrate a possible connection between religion and sports.

Sample

The faces of the players were young, but the perfection of their equipment, the gleaming shoes and helmets and the immaculate pants and jerseys, the solemn ritual that was attached to almost everything, made them seem like boys going off to fight a war for the benefit of someone else, unwitting sacrifices to a strange and powerful god. (11)

STEP 3

For each quotation, story, or description, write a one-paragraph explanation (based on the introduction) of why you chose that quotation, story, or description. How does it illustrate a possible connection between religion and sport? Make sure you indicate which definition of religion you are referencing.

Sample

This quotation illustrates the potential of sport to function as religion. It includes several of the elements Ninian Smart defined as aspects of religion: belief ("a strange and powerful god"), rituals (sacrifice and other elements defined here as "solemn"), material objects ("gleaming shoes and helmets and immaculate pants and jerseys"), and belonging ("for the benefit of someone else"). The reference to going off to fight a war could connect to Robert Bellah's concept of civil religion and its analogies to patriotism.

STEP 4

Using the arguments against viewing sport as religion, explain why some might argue against the segment you chose.

Sample

Higgs argues that sports represent everything that was wrong with ancient religions: violence, sacrifice, and the connection to war. All those factors are present in this quotation. Guttmann suggests these links to ancient religions that might be represented by sport in ancient times no longer matter in the highly corporatized world of sport today. This example is more about the connection between football and war rather than football and religion.

STEP 5

After having done this exercise for each quotation, story, or description you've chosen, you decide. Having viewed the argument from different perspectives, are there sufficient examples in *FNL* that point to Mojo as a religion in this case study? Use specific examples in making your final argument.

Part 2 in class

STEP 1

Meet in pairs and compare your quotations, stories, and descriptions. If you used examples that you didn't have in common, describe them to each other. Look at the ones you found in common and compare your conclusions about them. Discuss the differences. Decide which of your examples make the best argument in favor of the connection between sport and religion and which make the best argument against the connection.

STEP 2

Each pair presents their best arguments.

ACTIVITY 2

STEP 1

Buzz Bissinger had no interest in the question of whether he was describing a religion or not. Yet it is clear that he uses language often associated with religion (sacrifice, ritual, God, saints, faith) to describe the Panthers and their loyal fans. Find five times Bissinger uses the term *religion*. For each instance, write a paragraph about what you think he means when he's using the term. Use the definitions you find in the introduction to do this part of the exercise.

STEP 2

Create 3 questions to ask Bissinger for a mock interview focused on the connection between sports and religion. Submit the questions you'd like to ask him about his views on this topic to the discussion board of your course's electronic Web site.

STEP 3

Pick out one question submitted by another student and answer it as if you were Bissinger. You may choose to do further research about him to find out more about his interests and attitudes about religion to inform your answer.

Extra Credit

Watch the film *Friday Night Lights*. List the scenes that you think have a religious dimension and explain why.

CASE 2

Oscar Pistorius and What It Means to Be Human

Fig. 2.1. Oscar Pistorius runs during the men's 4 x 400 meter in the Olympic Stadium at the 2012 Summer Olympics, London. AP Photo/Lee Jin-man.

GOAL: To apply our understanding of sport as a religion to the values connected to human embodiment, justice, and fairness.

Oscar Pistorius achieved international fame in 2012 when he became the first double amputee runner to compete in the Olympics. He had already won multiple races in the Paralympics against mostly single amputee athletes and sought to test his abilities at this next level. Whether or not Pistorius would be allowed to compete against able-bodied athletes on his "cheetah legs" was initially adjudicated by the International Association of Athletics Federations (IAAF), which passed a rule in 2007 against allowing runners to use devices with springs or wheels in anticipation, it was widely believed, of Pistorius's contemplated goal. The ruling was later overturned on appeal by the Court of Arbitration of Sport, paving the way for Pistorius to compete in London.

Then, at the height of his fame, on Valentine's Day 2013, Pistorius killed his girlfriend, Reeva Steenkamp, claiming that he mistook her for an intruder. The trial lasted for a year and was closely watched as people around the world (and especially in South Africa) questioned whether Pistorius could still be a hero. Although judge Thokozile Masipa ruled that the act was not premeditated, she did find him guilty of culpable homicide and another firearms-related offense.

Whether or not sports is a religion, as a society we often ask religious questions in the context of sports. Pistorius's case lends itself to thinking through ultimate questions as expressed in two of the dimensions of religion outlined by Ninian Smart (see the introduction): the ethical/legal and the doctrinal/philosophical. What does it mean to be human? Is there such a thing as normal? Natural? Is it right to sort human beings into different categories based on age, gender, or physical ability for sports competitions? How do we decide what is just? What is fair? What makes someone a hero? Is hero a category for a man who is convicted of the reckless use of firearms that resulted in someone's death?

Oscar Pistorius was born in 1986 and raised in Johannesburg, South Africa. Born without a fibula in either leg, he would never be able to walk. His parents decided to have doctors amputate his legs below the knee when he was eleven months old in order to permit him to walk using prosthetic devices. His parents divorced when he was young, and his mother died when he was fifteen. As a child he played sports including tennis, water polo, and rugby. In his autobiography he describes how a rugby injury led to the start of a career as a sprinter in 2004. Pistorius claimed not to have any interest in running; his original goal was to rehabilitate so he could return to playing rugby. But when he was fitted with running blades that allowed him to run swiftly (as compared to the ones he used as a child), he discovered both his great ability, and the joy of movement. His talent was such that he soon outgrew the blades he was using and so was fitted with a newly designed J-shaped prosthetic manufactured by an Icelandic manufacturer, Össur, called the "flex-foot Cheetah." Using this device, Pistorius quickly claimed a new nickname, Blade Runner and status as "the fastest man on no legs." Although he doesn't describe himself as religious, he identifies as a Christian and was close to his mother, who herself was most devout. One of his two tattoos is the verse from 1 Corinthians 9:26–27, "I do not run like a man running aimlessly." His career as a runner took on passion and purpose.

Although Pistorius was classified as T43 (double amputee), he competed and won events in the T44 (single amputee) category in Paralympic contests beginning in 2004. He won the bronze medal in the 100 meter event and the gold medal (and a world record) in the 200 meter in Athens in 2004, and gold in the 100, 200, and 400 meter events in Beijing in 2008. He continued to compete in the 2012 Paralympics, winning silver in the 200 meter, and gold in the 400 meter and 400 meter relay, all against single amputees.

In 2005 he began running in able-bodied national and international competitions as well. Pistorius contemplated competing in the 2008 Beijing Olympics, but in 2007 the IAAF banned "any technical device that incorporates springs, wheels or any other element that provides a user with an advantage over another athlete not using such a device."

The concern, as it was expressed, was about a "slippery slope." If the prosthetic devices were allowed, as one official put it, someday someone would want to "fly with something on their back." It was even suggested that people might amputate their legs to gain an advantage. Although the IAAF did not say so, it is widely believed that this ruling was meant to keep Pistorius out of the Olympics, as word had gotten around that the "cheetah legs" he was running on might present an unfair advantage. The IAAF denied that the rule was created for Pistorius, then requested that Pistorius undergo scientific testing to determine whether the prosthetics did create an unfair advantage. Pistorius agreed to take part in the tests conducted by Peter Bruggemann, a renowned professor of biomechanics in Cologne, Germany. Bruggemann determined that the devices did provide an unfair advantage because the prosthetics cut down on the mechanical work required and Pistorius did not have to use as much energy to propel his legs as an able-bodied athlete does. Based on these findings, Pistorius was disqualified from the 2008 Summer Olympics in Beijing. Pistorius appealed the decision to the Court of Arbitration for Sport in Switzerland. To that court, Pistorius brought testimony from a second series of tests he underwent under the supervision of scientists from MIT, the University of Colorado, and Rice University in Houston, Texas. Here scientists ran other tests based on a larger number of variables including leg movements and oxygen consumption. They concluded that although Pistorius's blades were mechanically different he remained physiologically similar to able-bodied runners. While the scientists themselves actually disagreed about whether the blades provided an advantage, they agreed that the evidence presented by Bruggemann's studies was not adequate to resolve the question and should not have determined his eligibility to compete.

Based on this additional evidence the court ruled in Pistorius's favor. The IAAF accepted the ruling for this specific case only, not ready to set a precedent that could open the door for other prosthetic devices. All the legal battles and laboratory testing left Pistorius with little training time, and he did not qualify in the 2008 trials. The IAAF also cautioned the South African Olympic committee not to select Pistorius for the 4x400 meter relay "for reasons of safety." He was not included on the team.

Pistorius set to work to prepare for the 2012 London Olympics. His extensive training paid off. He became the first amputee runner to compete at an Olympic games, although not the first person with disabilities to compete at the Olympics. George Eyser won a gold medal in gymnastics for the United States in 1904 on a wooden leg. Neroli Fairhall from New Zealand competed in archery in the 1984 Olympics in a wheelchair. Legally blind U.S. runner Marla Runyan competed in the 1,500 meter race in 2000. Pistorius, however, was the most famous. He carried the South African flag at the 2012 closing ceremonies. He was one of *Time* magazine's one hundred most influential people in 2008 and again in 2012. He had signed on for many sponsorship deals, including Nike and Thierry Mugler. He was a leading proponent of the Mineseeker Foundation; a charitable organization that raises awareness about the victims of landmines to which he contributed extensively in publicity and funding.

Before his trial, Pistorius was a "cipher" viewed simultaneously as

- a runner who was trying to do his best,
- a cheater who used an unfair advantage to gain commercial success,
- a role model for people with disabilities who made able-bodied people rethink the notion of disability as a deficit,
- a "techno-human hybrid" who raised profound issues about the boundaries between categories of human and technological.

After he admitted to committing a homicide, views of Pistorius changed. The trial lasted almost a year, received worldwide media coverage, and was televised in its entirety. The presiding judge, Thokozile Masipa, was only the second black woman with an appointment to the high court in the history of South Africa. The case gripped the nation and raised questions about its culture of racism, fear, and violence. When he was accused, Pistorius lost his sponsorships and forfeited opportunities to compete as a runner. The judge's verdict of culpable homicide rather than murder continued to be widely debated, as was Pistorius' character. Is he a reckless user of firearms? A frightened person with impaired judgment? A man made vulnerable by his disability? A victim of circumstance? Another athlete who got away with intimate partner violence?

ACTIVITY

CHOOSING ETHICAL PRINCIPLES TO HELP US SORT OUT THE QUESTIONS RAISED BY THE PISTORIUS CASE

The Pistorius case challenges us to confront a variety of difficult ethical questions. The goal of this activity is to develop answers to those questions guided by values from the world of religion and sports. For example, some ethicists have suggested that Pistorius's prostheses put him in the category of *post* or *trans*human. Theologian Tracy Trothen has argued that the standard for defining what it means to be human should be the idea, found in Abrahamic traditions, that human beings are created in God's image. What human characteristics are central to that definition? Do Pistorius's high-tech prostheses put him in a different category?

Other religious values could also be used to deal with dilemmas raised by this case. When it comes to the question of whether it was fair to allow Pistorius to compete in the Olympics against able-bodied runners (or single amputees), we can look to a value found in all the world's religions, the Golden Rule—that we should not do to others what we wouldn't want done to us. Or we could use a value derived more specifically from Buddhist teachings, which emphasizes compassion above all. Sports, too, have values that can help us in our deliberations, including the main criterion for judging Olympic virtue, "Higher, Faster, Stronger." Other values associated with the Olympics that could be applied to questions raised by the Pistorius case include creating a level playing field and welcoming diversity.

For each set of questions that follow, select one of these values (creation in God's image; the Golden Rule; the principle of compassion; higher, faster, stronger; creating a level playing field; welcoming diversity; or another value you've discussed in class). Explain why you chose that value and how that value helped you sort out the ethical dilemmas. The resource list contains a variety of articles and books that will help you formulate your response.

QUESTIONS

- Does Pistorius have an "unfair advantage" running on his cheetah legs? Does it matter if he's running against able-bodied athletes or single amputees? Is running on prosthetic devices the same as running on human legs? Is it the same race? As scientific evidence was inconclusive, how is justice to be determined in this case?
- Should the burden have been placed on Pistorius to pay for his tests and trials? Should athletes be given the presumption of good faith?
- The IAAF argued that if Pistorius slipped during a race his prosthetics could have posed a danger to the other able-bodied runners. Is the safety of other athletes a relevant factor?
- Sports divide athletes into competitive groups based on age, sex, weight, and physical ability. For many years, Olympic athletes have been subjected to tests to determine whether they fit into the "proper" gender category. Should there be separate classifications for these embodied characteristics? Does the Pistorius case blur the boundaries? How do these considerations affect standards of fairness?
- Is not being able to do something you'd like to be able to do a good definition of disability? Isn't everyone impaired in some way?
- Is Pistorius transhuman or posthuman? Is he a cyborg" (a human-machine combination)? Are prosthetic devices central to his identity? What is a biologically pure identity? How do we determine what is normal or natural? Is any elite athlete normal? How do you distinguish between the real and the artificial? Is there such a thing as "technophobic stigmatism"? Does it matter if technological devices are internal (an artificial hip) versus external (prosthetic legs)? Does an "enhanced human" change the nature of sport? Is this a case about the value of technological progress that will improve on humans through genetic engineering, artificial intelligence, robotics, nanotechnology, virtual reality? Will all athletes be transhuman in the future? Will technologically enhanced Paralympics make Olympics look boring?

- Do sports magnify the problem of disabilities because of its emphasis on perfect bodies? Why might able-bodied people be afraid of athletes with disabilities? What does it say about human perfection if the disabled body can win?
- What is the relationship between technological devices and "doping"? How do you decide if achievement is based on training, talent, or technology? What is the right combination of these factors? Is there such a thing as purity, and should it be a value? How can you tell the difference between a fair and an unfair advantage?
- Is the difference between therapeutic measures that repair a body to its "normal" state and performance enhancements that take the body outside its "normal" limits theologically or ethically relevant to this case? Where do you draw the line between therapy and enhancement? Should geographic or class advantages also be factored in? Should other endowments like height or leg length? What about access to good nutrition, coaches, psychologists? How about access to equipment, clothing, or surgery? What's the relationship between these enhancements and pharmaceuticals or genetic manipulations?
- Should someone who has been tried for murder still be considered a hero? Can he still be a role model for people with disabilities? For the nation of South Africa? Should we continue to study the case of Oscar Pistorius in relation to the issues of sports and disability, or has he disgraced himself? Do you agree with the verdict and sentence that was handed down?

FINAL QUESTION FOR CLASS DISCUSSION

- Does this case lend credence to the idea that sports are a holy venue where human beings can prove their value and merit and have an opportunity for spiritual expression?

RESOURCES

Burkett, Brendan, Mike McNamee, and Wolfgang Potthast. "Shifting Boundaries in Sports Technology and Disability: Equal Rights or Unfair Advantage in the Case of Oscar Pistorius?" *Disability and Society* 26.5 (2011): 643–654.

Charlish, Peter and Dr. Stephen Riley. "Should Oscar Run?" *Fordham Intellectual Property, Media & Entertainment Law Journal* 18 (2008): 929–957.

Crincoli, Shawn. "You Can Only Race If You Can't Win? The Curious Cases of Oscar Pistorius and Caster Semenya." *Texas Review of Entertainment and Sports Law* 12.2 (2011): 133–187.

Edwards, S. D. "Should Oscar Pistorius Be Excluded from the 2008 Olympic Games?" *Sport, Ethics and Philosophy* 2.2 (2008): 112–125.

Eveleth, Rose. "Should Oscar Pistorius's Prosthetic Legs Disqualify Him from the Olympics?" *Scientific American* (July 24, 2012). http://www.scientific american.com/article/scientists-debate-oscar-pistorius-prosthetic-legs -disqualify-him-olympics/.

Hood, Marlowe. "Born to Run." *IEEE Spectrum June 2005.* http://spectrum.ieee.org/ biomedical/bionics/running-againstthe-wind.

Jones, Carwyn. "Oscar Pistorus, the Paralympics, and Issues of Fair Competition." In Sandra Spickard Prettyman and Brian Lampman, eds., *Learning Culture Through Sports: Perspectives on Society and Organized Sports,* 238–250. 2d ed. Lanham, MD: Rowman and Littlefield, 2011.

—— and Cassie Wilson. "Defining Advantage and Athletic Performance: The Case of Oscar Pistorius." *European Journal of Sport Science* 9.2 (2009): 125–131.

Klein, Shawn. "Sports Ethicist." http://sportsethicist.com/category/oscar-pistorius/ March 1, 2013.

Longman, Jeré. "An Amputee Sprinter: Is He Disabled or Too-Abled?" *New York Times,* May 15, 2007.

Magdalinski, Tara. *Sport, Technology and the Body: the Nature of Performance.* New York: Routledge, 2009.

Marcellini, Anne, Sylvain Ferez, Damien Issanchou, Eric De Léséleuc, and Mike McNamee. "Challenging Human and Sporting Boundaries: The Case of Oscar Pistorius." *Performance Enhancement and Health* 1 (2012): 3–9.

Moss, Norman E. and Fiona Moola. "'Bladerunner or Boundary Runner'? Oscar Pistorius, Cyborg Transgressions and Strategies of Containment." *Sport in Society: Cultures, Commerce, Media, Politics* 14.9 (2011): 1265–1279.

Nordenfelt, L. "On the Notions of Disability and Handicap." *Social Welfare* 2 (1993): 17–24.

Pistorius, Oscar. *Blade Runner.* London: Virgin, 2009.

Sokolove, Mark. "The Fast Life of Oscar Pistorius." *New York Times Magazine,* January 18, 2012.

Swartz, Leslie and Brian Watermeyer. "Cyborg Anxiety: Oscar Pistorius and the Boundaries of What It Means to Be Human." *Disability and Society* 23.2 (2008): 187–190.

Triviño, José Luis Pérez. "Cyborgsportpersons: Between Disability and Enhancement." *Physical Culture and Sport Studies Research* 57 (2013): 12–21.

Trothen, Tracy. "Redefining Human, Redefining Sport: The Imago Dei and Genetic Modification Techniques." In Donald Deardorff II and John White, eds., *The Image of God in the Human Body: Essays on Christianity and Sports,* 217–234. Lewiston, NY: Edwin Mellen, 2008.

——. "The Technoscience Enhancement Debate in Sports: What's Religion Got to Do with It?" In Nick J. Watson and Andrew Parker, eds., *Sports and Christianity: Historical and Contemporary Perspectives,* 207–224. New York: Routledge, 2013.

Van Hilvoorde, Ivo and Laurens Landeweerd. "Enhancing Disabilities: Transhumanism Under the Veil of Inclusion." *Disability and Rehabilitation* 32.26 (2010): 2222–2227.

——. "Disability or Extraordinary Talent—Francesco Lentini (Three Legs) Versus Oscar Pistorius (No Legs)." *Sport, Ethics, and Philosophy* 2.2 (2008): 97–111.

PART 2

DOES RELIGION HAVE A PLACE IN SPORTS, OR SPORTS IN RELIGION?

In this section we will look at a series of cases to try to understand what happens when traditional religions play a part in sports. The cases, which come from different parts of the world, ask whether there are limits to the intersection between religion and sports. Case 3 examines the connection that is often made between archery and Zen Buddhism. We look at whether archery really is central to Zen practice or if it was merely used by Westerners (and some Japanese interpreters) as a way to explain Zen to Europeans and enhance Japanese national pride. Case 4 looks at what happens when teams play for religious institutions. The women's basketball team at the Immaculata College in Pennsylvania took their Catholic affiliation to new heights, which involved teachers and administrators creating prayers for their success. Case 5 takes us to Africa where virtually every football (soccer) team uses juju (magic and witchcraft) to help them gain good results. Here we ask about the role of religion as an aid to sports success and compare the African situation to some American and European practices. Case 6 questions the well-entrenched phenomenon of Baseball Chapel, the organization that provides Christian prayer services for all Major League Baseball teams on Sundays before games. We'll look at whether or not this practice infringes on the rights of those who don't want to participate and what accommodations need to be made to ensure everyone's freedom of religion in the world of sports.

CASE 3

Zen and Archery in Japan

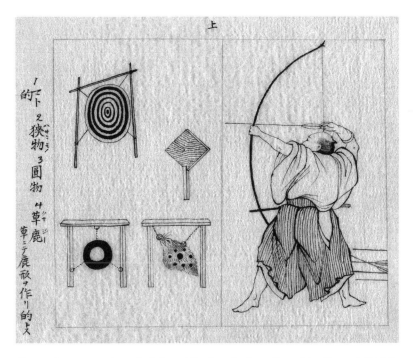

Fig. 3.1. Japanese archer, 1878. In public domain. http://en.wikipedia.org/wiki/File:Japanese_archer_1878b.jpg.

GOAL: to understand the complex relationship between Zen Buddhism and archery.

Archery is a martial art that was practiced in many ancient cultures, including Egypt, Greece, and indigenous cultures of Africa and the Americas. It was also popular in China and Japan at least a thousand years ago. It has been utilized in warfare, hunting, ceremonial ritual, and as a sport in all those cultures. Firearms replaced the bow and arrow in most places in the sixteenth century, so archery's role in warfare and hunting was reduced drastically at that point in time. In most cultures it remained a sport and in some a spiritual and ritual activity.

Until modern times, archery in Japan was known by two terms that were interchangeable: *kyūjutsu* (the art of the bow) and *kyūdō* (the way of the bow). The suffix -jutsu emphasizes the technical skill while the suffix -*do* emphasizes the spiritual path, or "the way." Today, *kyūdō* is the more commonly used term, preferred by Japanese teachers to emphasize the spiritual rather than the martial dimensions of its physical arts.

Archaeologists have found Japanese hunting bows that date back to at least the fourth century BCE and were used as military weapons from the third century BCE. Japanese archery is unique because of the use of the long bow (*yumi*) that is at least seven feet in length and gripped not in the center, but in the lower half. The bow, made of wood and bamboo since medieval times, is treated as a sacred object and was believed to chase away evil spirits. The spiritual dimension of archery came to Japan through China in ancient times, based on Confucian practices that imbued it with moral meaning. For the archer to shoot successfully required a pure spirit and the willingness to accept responsibility for failure based on moral discipline. Archery was conducted in a ceremonial manner, and was meant to train both the mind and the body. It was passed down through schools (*ryū*) where ceremonial form was highly valued. The twelfth-century teacher Ogasawara Nagakiyo (1162–1242) taught a spiritually oriented archery whose traditions were lost and then revived in the seventeenth century.

Kyūdō incorporated ceremonial etiquette and spiritual training that might have been influenced by Buddhism. More militaristic and competitive versions of archery were also popular in the Tokugawa period (1603–1868). There were temple competitions (*tōshiya*) that were formalized and ceremonial events. These were public and important national rituals. Records kept are some of the oldest accounts of sporting events ever documented.[1]

When the Meiji Restoration began in Japan (1868), its leaders sought to eliminate ancient customs in an effort to modernize and fit in with Western cultures. A new state cult, called Shinto, was established, redefining old customs and attributing divinity to the emperor. Buddhism and other traditional practices were persecuted. Buddhist temples were destroyed, and monks and nuns forced to leave their monasteries. *Kyūdō* was among the activities that were devalued in the sweep to modernity, and shooting was relegated to an amusement and an opportunity for gambling that was not considered respectable.

Buddhists were among those who sought to revive old traditions and worked against odds to keep traditional Japanese spirituality alive through the avenues of martial arts, painting, tea ceremonies, and poetry. Eventually, martial arts, including *kyūdō,* were officially welcomed and returned to the curriculum of government sponsored schools as vehicles of spiritual education with Western elements of modern sport incorporated. In 1895 the government created an organization to oversee *kyūdō* and other martial arts, the Dai Nippon Butokukai (the Greater Japan Martial Virtues Society). The aim was to standardize practice and sponsor tournaments that would increase the popularity of these ancient practices. Tournaments were quite successful, but it was difficult to standardize *kyūdō,* as the many varieties that existed in the past were inspirations for many new versions of the sport, some more spiritually focused than others. The interest of the Butokukai was not in the spiritual elements but rather in *kyūdō* as a vehicle for physical training and to provide a pleasant way to pass the time.

Nevertheless, former archery specialists established new *kyūdō* organizations and created new styles that combined elements of Western-type archery with the traditional Japanese versions that were connected not only to sports as physical education but also as spiritual discipline.

Honda Toshizane (1836–1917) was the best known of these teachers. His disciples were Ohira Zenzo (1874–1952) and Awa Kenzo (1880–1939). Both were influenced by (modern) Buddhist and spiritual teachings and both created philosophies of archery using Zen terminology. Ohira established the Greater Japan Institute for Awakened Archery and called himself the Shooting Buddha. Awa invented his own version of archery, which he called Daishadōkyō, "Teaching of the Great Way of Shooting," based on a mystical experience he had in 1927 that he called the great explosion. Although Awa began as a skilled archer, his mystical experience led him to teach that once skills were acquired the archer should go beyond to find the shot's "true nature." That could only happen if the archer put his or her whole being ("an entire lifetime") into each shot. To Awa, Daishadōkyō was a unique path. He was not trained in Zen Buddhism, did not completely approve of Zen practices and teachings, and didn't see his way leading to *satori,* the Zen term for "enlightenment." He did not equate his "Great Way" with Zen, but he did use Zen terminology that was popular at the time to explain some of his ideas. Awa's teachings were ridiculed by many in Japan, and Daishadōkyō ended with his death since he had no disciples.[2] But he is well known today because he became the teacher of the man responsible for the widespread connections between *kyūdō* and Zen, Eugen Herrigel (1884–1955), author of *Zen in the Art of Archery.*[3]

If you do a quick Internet search for "Zen in (or Zen and) the art of" you will be dazzled by the variety of options you will find to instruct you in all sorts of things from the SATs to fly fishing.[4] The term *Zen in the art of* originated in Herrigel's 1948 text. It is the basis of all the others, including Robert Pirsig's perhaps now better-known *Zen and the Art of Motorcycle Maintenance.* The complex connection between Zen and archery lies at the heart of this tale. As you can see from the history sketched here, *kyūdō* had spiritual and ceremonial aspects from ancient times but was never primarily associated with Zen Buddhism. How Herrigel persuaded an entire world that Awa taught him Zen archery is a great story that we know because of the scholarly curiosity and painstaking research of a Japanese professor of engineering, Shoji Yamada. Before Yamada's revelations, published in 2001, Herrigel's mystical interpretation of Zen and its deep connection to archery in Japan were often accepted as the truth both in Japan and in the West.[5] Now they are generally regarded as an invented tradition. How that came to pass is an interesting story.

Herrigel, a German philosophy professor, taught in Japan from 1924–1929. He had mystical inclinations, and was influenced by the teachings of the great medieval Catholic teacher, Meister Eckhart. As was common in his time, Herrigel believed there were universal principles that defined religion, and therefore he assumed that learning the mystical traditions of Japan would lead to a deeper understanding of all mysticism. Herrigel went to Japan looking to enrich his connection to the spiritual. During this era, Zen Buddhism had become popular in the West (and particularly in the United States and Germany). It is likely that Herrigel was influenced by the teachings of D. T. Suzuki, the Japanese philosopher who brought his own interpretation of Zen Buddhism to the West. Suzuki popularized the notion that Zen was at the center of Japanese culture. A combination of Herrigel's mystical interests and the influence of Suzuki's philosophy were likely the reasons that Herrigel wanted to study Zen while he was living in Japan.

But Herrigel did not seek out a Zen master. Yamada compares him to another Western academic, Harvard Japanologist R. B. Acker, who lived in Japan from 1933 to 1937. Acker was interested in *kyūdō* and wrote a book about it, *The Fundamentals of Japanese Archery*, which was published in 1937. Acker was also interested in Zen and lived for a time at a temple designed to welcome Westerners. There Acker ate simple meals, meditated, and chanted along with the monks. Although quite familiar with Zen and Japanese archery, he only sparingly referred to Zen in his work. He noted Zen influences on archery (for example, the importance of breathing while shooting) but did not see Zen and archery as fundamentally connected.

Herrigel, on the other hand, took up archery as a vehicle to understand Japanese mysticism. Like Acker, he understood that he could not access the secrets of this Asian tradition intellectually, but only through experience. Nevertheless, he did not spend any time in a Buddhist monastery. His friends at the university suggested that learning one of the arts (poetry, painting, tea ceremonies, or martial arts) would be a good way to achieve his goal. Thinking that his background as a marksman would help him, he chose archery. A mutual friend, Komachiya, introduced Herrigel to the mystic archer Awa in 1926. Awa at first refused to teach him, having had bad experiences with Westerners before. But he was persuaded when Komachiya agreed to serve as a translator. Herrigel worked with Awa for three years and in 1929 returned to Germany to teach philosophy at the University of Erlangen and continue his spiritual archery practice while he wrote about his experience in Japan.

Yamada documents that Herrigel joined the National Socialist Party in 1933 and remained a member through the Nazi era. Of course, his refusal to join the party would have resulted in reprisals for him and his university. Nonetheless, the fact is chilling. Whether or not he had fascist leanings or harbored antisemitic tendencies (which he later denied), this fact (and that his Nazi affiliation had been omitted from his biographies) forms part of this story, although it had been suppressed in the past.

Upon his return to Germany, Herrigel gave a lecture about his experience of learning archery with Awa that was published in 1936. In the lecture he did not connect the experience with Zen. But in 1938 Suzuki published *Zen and Japanese Culture*, and reading it changed Herrigel's views. Herrigel's next version of the story, *Zen in the Art of Archery*, was published in German in 1948. Five years later the book was translated into English and into Japanese two years after that. It became quite popular. It described the experience Herrigel had with Awa as based on Zen Buddhism precisely in terms of Suzuki's understanding. Suzuki provided a brief introduction to the book where he gave his blessing to Herrigel's interpretation. "In this wonderful little book, Mr. Herrigel, a German philosopher who came to Japan and took up the practice of archery toward an understanding of Zen, gives an illuminating account of his own experience. Through his expression, the Western reader will find a more familiar manner of dealing with what very often must seem to be a strange and somewhat unapproachable Eastern experience" (ix). Although Suzuki later claimed he never believed that Herrigel understood Zen at all,[6] this imprimatur verified Herrigel's bona fides, and the connection between Zen and archery was established.

But as documented by Yamada, Awa was a practitioner of his own religion, Daishadōkyō, and was not trained in Zen. Furthermore, the mystical experience that Herrigel described and that captured worldwide attention may have been based on mistranslations. However, Herrigel explained them lyrically, and the short book is definitely worth reading, so you can gain direct experience of why this work, still in print, remains popular and spawned a whole industry of "Zen and the art of" literature. Whether what Herrigel experienced through accepting "the great doctrine" was Zen or Daishadōkyō or his own Eckhart-based mystical union with God, Herrigel indeed describes a deeply spiritual experience achieved through the discipline of archery.

Herrigel's book explained how through archery he could enter the mystical realm in a way that couldn't happen in intellectual study. The Zen approach to archery was to become one with the experience, to reach a state of shooting the arrow with "effortless effort"—difficult to describe and even harder to do. Herrigel explained that his lessons began with respecting and holding the bow. Awa judged him a failure at this first lesson, so the lessons took a step backward. Awa began again, teaching Herrigel how to breathe and relax his body without the bow in hand. This practiced breathing and relaxation is central to all types of meditation and a key part of the spiritual dimension of Japanese archery from ancient times. Even those who deny any connection between Zen and archery note the necessity of correct breathing. Herrigel recounted the words of Awa as he remembered them: "That's just the trouble, you make an effort to think about it. Concentrate entirely on your breathing, as if you had nothing else to do!" (25). He recalled asking the translator Komachiya why Awa didn't simply start the lessons with learning how to breathe, and his friend explained that great teaching consisted of allowing the student to fail first. According to this philosophy, in order to succeed you must know how it feels to fail.

Yamada's research revealed that the two main experiences Herrigel claimed as moments of enlightenment (a perfect shot Awa made in the dark and learning what it means to say "it shoots" rather than "I shoot it") were based on misunderstandings. Herrigel wanted to share his new understanding that "effortless effort" could only be achieved without reference to the self. He related the following conversation:

One day I asked the Master: "How can the shot be loosed if 'I' do not do it?"

"It shoots," he replied.

"I have heard you say that several times before, so let me put it another way: How can I wait self-obliviously for the shot if 'I' am no longer there?"

"'It' waits at the highest tension."

"And who or what is this 'It'?"

"Once you have understood that, you will have no further need of me."

(58)

Yamada deduced that "it shoots" was not the great Zen insight of selflessness that Herrigel thought he was gaining, but a simple statement, akin to the English "good shot." While this exposes Herrigel's poor communication with Awa, the point remains that Herrigel "got" the basic idea of letting go of ego and self that was central to doing archery in a spiritual way, even if he could not achieve it.

Yamada also suggested that Herrigel missed the point of Awa's lesson of shooting in the dark. Without taking aim (or seeking a goal), Awa shot two arrows into the center of the target in a darkened room. The second landed in the nock of the first. According to Yamada, while the first arrow landed perfectly, having the second land in the first, which awed and amazed Herrigel, was likely a coincidence. It also would have been a source of shame for Awa as archers were not supposed to damage their equipment. Herrigel translated Awa's response, "It is not 'I' who must be given credit for this shot. 'It' shot and 'It' made the hit. Let us bow to the goal as before the Buddha" (67). Since the translator was not present, Yamada argues that Herrigel supplied his own interpretation—this is enlightenment—rather than simply what Awa was trying to communicate—this is a coincidence.

Yamada concludes that Herrigel presented "empty signs" and no real understanding of Zen, beyond the psychological insights of breathing and letting go of ego, and that Suzuki himself was aware of this. Zen Buddhism without monastics, sitting meditation, a tradition of koans (parables), and satori (enlightenment) was only a shadow of Zen. But in the aftermath of World War II Japan wanted to present itself to the world in the best possible light (presumably Germany did as well), and this view of archery as representing the deeply meaningful and mystical side of Japanese culture identified as Zen was welcomed and celebrated.

In 1949 the All Nippon Kyudo Federation was formed to replace the Butokukai, which had been dissolved. The role of the new federation was to promote *kyūdō*, organize archery meets, and once again attempt to standardize rules. Part of the goal was to promote *kyūdō* as a way of instilling the virtues of discipline and hard work. They made an effort to incorporate old ceremonial values while bringing *kyūdō* up to date. Archery became an Olympic sport at the 1964 Tokyo games. Even the Westernized form of *kyūdō* could not compete with new Western archery equipment and training, and the Japanese archers did not win medals. So for *kyūdō* to be presented as a spiritual discipline rather than a sport certainly saved face for the Japanese hosts.

ACTIVITY

Read these two accounts of practitioners of *kyūdō* in the United States and respond to the following questions.

ACCOUNT 1

In 1988 Rebecca Hsu was a junior in college and a member of the Columbia University archery team. She was ranked first among all U.S. women indoor collegiate archers. She attracted media attention for her outstanding play, which led Columbia to an undefeated season. In an interview with Joe Tintle, a reporter for *Newsday*, Hsu attributed her success to the lessons she learned from Al Lizzio, her coach, and also to reading Herrigel's *Zen in the Art of Archery*. What she learned from the book was to "focus on herself, not the target." He reported that she "empties her mind of everything unrelated to the sport. She thinks only about technique. Then she fits the arrow onto the bowstring, raises the bow, draws it back and releases it." Rather than aim, she separates herself from distractions and concentrates on her body, using the techniques of visualization and the deep breathing she learned from Herrigel's account. She never looks at the target but "feels the arrow . . . whether I see it hit or not." She explained further: "What's the point of concentrating on what's down there [the target]. After all, nothing is going on." Her teammates referred to her as a "shooting machine" and admired her detachment and concentration.[7]

ACCOUNT 2

In 1975 Koen Mishima founded the Los Angeles Kyūdō Kai (Club). Mishima, who was the spiritual leader of the local Higashi Hongwanji Buddhist Temple, wanted to revive the tradition of *kyūdō* that flourished in the neighborhood known as Little Tokyo from 1916 through World War II. It ended when Japanese residents were sent to internment camps, interrupting their lives and destroying their cultural practices. In 1993 Iris Yokoi, a reporter for the *Los Angeles Times*, interviewed Hirokazu Kosaka, an instructor at the center, to learn about how he was reviving the practice of *kyūdō*.

Yokoi went to the center for the interview. There she observed the "small group of Zen archers" dressed in white shirts, black kimono pants, and white socks. They began their session with meditation, reading of Buddhist sutras, and archery practice. Kosaka, she explained, taught them to attend to their breathing and created a peaceful and solemn environment for their weekly sessions.

When they began their shooting practice, Kosaka provided silent instruction, but during their tea break he reminded them: "Just be—don't think . . . If you tighten your muscles, you will never be able to keep your breath in. Try to think about nothing. . . . Don't try to hit the target, 'shoot yourself.'"

When Kosaka told Yokoi that he was critical of Herrigel's book, the journalist expressed surprise. Kosaka was clear that "Western egos" could not understand the practice and even called Herrigel's book "dangerous." He complained of many Westerners who came to his center and soon left because they didn't have the discipline or understanding to follow through.[8]

QUESTIONS

- Explain how Rebecca Hsu's observations reflect what you learned from this case about Zen and archery. What factors are you considering when making this judgment? Are there elements of her story that don't correlate with Herrigel's account?
- Write Rebecca Hsu a letter explaining what you would want her to know about Yamada's criticisms of *Zen in the Art of Archery*. Do you think having that information would change her archery technique?
- Describe the ways Kosaka's understanding of *kyūdō* differs from Eugen Herrigel's views.
- Create a Twitter post by Eugen Herrigel. Write responses for Kosaka and Rebecca Hsu.
- Stevens quotes Awa as saying: "The way of the bow is not a religion. It is the teaching of Great Nature, a state of mind that transcends religion."[9] What is Awa's understanding of religion? Do you understand his teaching as different from religion? Is it a fusion of archery and spirituality as some claim?

CASE 4

O God of Players

PRAYER AND WOMEN'S BASKETBALL AT A CATHOLIC COLLEGE

Fig. 4.1. Sister Regina Socorro Kovalik, I. H. M. under the basket at Alumnae Hall, 1974, the cover image from *O God of Players*. Courtesy Ross Watson.

GOAL: To examine the role of Catholic ritual and belief in the lives of the young women who played basketball at Immaculata College.

READ: Chapter 4, "Praying for the Team," in *O God of Players: The Story of the Immaculata Mighty Macs* by Julie Byrne (New York: Columbia University Press, 2003), 113–141.

When I moved to Philadelphia in the early 1970s, one of the biggest and most surprising news stories was about the "Mighty Macs" women's basketball team from nearby Immaculata College. The Mighty Macs (not the diminutively named "Lady" Owls of Temple University or the Lionettes of Penn State as some women's teams were and are still called) won the first Women's National Collegiate Basketball Championship in 1972 and went on to win the next two as well. Inevitably and largely in response to Title IX, which shifted money and attention to women's sports, larger and better-funded schools developed strong teams, and the Mighty Macs could not sustain their place at the top of women's college basketball, but they were there at the beginning.

Julie Byrne's *O God of Players* explains that the success of the Immaculata team of the 1970s was not really a surprise. Young Catholic women grew up in Philadelphia playing basketball—with their brothers at home, in recreation centers, Catholic Youth Organization clubs (after 1940), and in Catholic high schools. Ninety percent of Catholic youth in the Philadelphia area were educated in Catholic schools, and the high schools were sex segregated, creating a comfortable environment in which girls' basketball flourished. The culture of competitive women's basketball was part and parcel of Catholic life in Philadelphia. The best players went on to play at Immaculata, a Catholic women's college run by the Immaculate Heart Sisters located in nearby Malvern, Pennsylvania. The school's administrators, especially Sister Mary of Lourdes McDevitt, the president from 1954–1972, were avid basketball fans and welcomed and supported the game. No men were involved. The team had no priests as chaplains, and the coaches and officials were all women. The coaches that revolutionized women's basketball at Immaculata, Jen Shillingford and Cathy Rush, were not even Catholic.

The story of the Mighty Macs, as Byrne tells it, challenges our notions that Catholic women were always submissive and repressed within the life of the church, even in Philadelphia, one of the most conservative dioceses in the United States. These young women were not rebels or radicals, and almost all continued a life of faith in the church, most as wives and mothers, some as nuns and Catholic educators. Byrne argues persuasively that looking at aspects of lived religion like this one gives us a more nuanced understanding of American Catholic life. As she puts it, "And a Catholic is a Catholic not only when she lights votive candles, but also when she plays basketball" (11).

Byrne shows that basketball at Immaculata was Catholic not only culturally but also religiously. She explains that sports, both for girls and boys in mid-twentieth century, are deeply connected to the Thomist values central to American Catholicism. Both men and women are obligated to perfect their immortal souls, and to do so necessitates perfecting the vessels (the human bodies) in which those souls are housed. The moral values that sport encourages—teamwork and leadership, discipline and perseverance—were also in keeping with Thomism, just as they were in sync with the values of muscular Christianity and the religion of sport. Chapter 4 of O God of Players, "Praying for the Team," takes a close look at how those beliefs were put into practice through ritual and is the subject of our case study. We will see if the wish Byrne expresses in her acknowledgments, "if this project conveys just a glimpse of God's hand in these women's lives—and in my life—it fulfills a purpose," resonates with you and your perception of the interconnections of religion and sport as manifest through the experience of the Mighty Macs.

ACTIVITIES

ACTIVITY 1

On pages 113–114 Byrne describes in detail how the Mighty Macs interpreted a loss they experienced on Ash Wednesday to Queens College in

1974 through the lens of their religious beliefs. List all the interpretations the players gave. Explain which ones were convincing and why. Were any of the explanations possible from other points of view? How might someone from another religion we have studied (Islam, Protestantism, Judaism, Native American tradition, Juju, Buddhism, or "the religion of sport") have interpreted the loss differently? Provide one example of how someone from a different religious tradition might interpret a loss on a religious holiday. What is your own personal view of this? Do you agree with Byrne's comment that "while faith infused basketball, so sometimes basketball talked back to faith"? (116). Why or why not?

ACTIVITY 2

Byrne focuses on the pregame prayer "O God of Players" (120–122). She explains that the origins of this prayer are unknown, but that players she interviewed for the book had memories of reciting it in Catholic high school contexts as well.

> O God of Players, hear our prayer
> To play this game and play it fair
> To compete, win, but if to lose
> Not to revile or to abuse
> But with understanding start again
> Give us the strength, O Lord. Amen

Analyze this prayer. You may include Byrne's ideas, but make sure you do some original thinking about it as well. Why do you think Byrne used it as the title of her book? What are its outstanding features? What values does it express? How would you describe its theology—what does it mean to call on the "God of Players"? Why do you think the women all remembered the words? What was the most important thing that this ritual gave the Mighty Mac team? Does it matter that it isn't especially "Catholic"?

Write your own pregame prayer. You may choose to use the same six-line format and rhyming scheme or some other poetic scheme (haiku, rap) that resonates for you. Analyze your prayer. What values does it express and what made you choose them? What kind of ritual would you create for your prayer?

ACTIVITY 3

Byrne describes their 1970s game rituals on pages 122–130. Compile a list. Why were these rituals important? Who did they benefit and why? Which is your favorite? Are there any of these rituals you already include in your sports life? Are there any you think would adapt well to your routines?

ACTIVITY 4

At the end of the chapter (136–141), Byrne gives voice to those who rejected the connections between Catholic religious beliefs and basketball rituals. List the reasons they give. Use their reasoning to reply to the proposition raised by a player on page 123:

> Why are we winning? Is it just because you're good, or is there a little bit of help from upstairs, that he is really behind you? And we all believed that . . . you have so much power behind you from the Almighty that you're doing as well as we are. . . . We always thought that we had a lot of help from the outside and it wasn't visible help.

Extra credit

How would you answer Byrne's question: "Does God enjoy basketball?" (136)?

CASE 5

Juju

WITCHCRAFT AND AFRICAN FOOTBALL

Fig. 5.1. Dumezulu Witchdoctor/Sangoma Spiritual adviser SA from the film *Kick the Lion*. All photography by Oliver G. Becker/Occasione Documentaries.

GOAL: To understand the role of witchcraft for football (soccer) teams on the African continent, and compare it to European and American "superstitions."

Juju is a term that is often used to describe the objects and activities associated with witchcraft in Africa. Juju is a complex set of rituals, which, when skillfully administered by juju specialists (also known as spiritual advisers) are thought to be capable of influencing the results of one of Africa's (and the world's) most popular activities, football (or soccer, as it's known in North America, but for this case study I will refer to it as football, as it is known around the world). Juju is not the same as "voodoo," although to English speakers the words sound alike.[1] Juju, properly done, increases a team's spiritual power. As the opposing team will also have employed juju in their preparations, a secondary goal is to defend players against the effects of the rituals performed by the opposing team's juju specialist. These juju rituals are understood to supplement the physical talents, techniques, and skills that are also necessary to win. No one believes that juju can make a team with inferior abilities beat a team that has trained harder and has more talent. But effective spiritual advisers can influence the outcome of a game—the dimension that is often, in our culture, understood as luck or chance—through their ritual ministrations. Juju has a role in other dimensions of life in African societies, such as dance contests and economic transactions, but its presence in African football is pervasive, and the two are often seen as inseparable. Because the outcome of sporting events like a football contest is always unpredictable, sports are inevitably a place where the human desire to control the results and explain the inexplicable comes into play. Juju provides explanations that are in keeping with the moral values of African Traditional Religions (ATR).

When people who have been raised in a culture like ours that is based on the model of scientific rationality encounter cultures where the efficacy of juju is taken for granted, we are puzzled and skeptical. The strange ritualized behaviors that coaches, players, and fans all around the world perform to help their teams win are labeled "superstitions" in the scientific worldview. These behaviors are assumed to have "only" a psychological impact as a placebo, if given any credence at all. Neurological researchers are studying this phenomenon, however, and they are coming to understand that the spiritual and psychological elements of preparation for sport may be less trivial in determining the outcome than a scientific model has predicted.

Although social scientists try to keep an open mind and accept the idea that other cultures are based on different models that are just as good as our own, we often find ourselves assuming that cultures that are based on a different mental model are wrong, primitive, or inferior. This is one effect of the belief in the independent validity of scientific truth and the legacy of the early anthropologists who, when attempting to describe other cultures neutrally, were often condescending about them.[2] In this case study I invite you to keep an open mind, to be curious instead of judgmental about the role of juju in football and how the concepts of African religion are neither better nor worse, simply different. The activities at the end of this case study will give you an opportunity to think through your own position on the topic.

When Christians and Muslims brought their religious traditions and values to Africa during the past two millennia, the indigenous populations incorporated their traditional belief systems into their understandings and practices of these world religions. The traditional religions practiced in Africa are sophisticated and complex, and I will only describe here some basic beliefs that are relevant to the connections between ATR and football. First, ATR has a very different understanding of the relationship between people who are alive today and the ancestors who came before. In ATR the spirit of the ancestors is manifest in everything in this world. The living must respect and venerate them, or we run the risk of failing to achieve the status of ancestor when we die. If we don't pay proper respect the ancestors will also get angry and cause troubles. But spiritual advisers (and witch doctors) can help us perform rituals that will put us back on the right track. They can also communicate with the ancestors to better understand their wishes and intentions for us in this world and protect us from the ancestors' displeasures made manifest in our world through our experiences of ill fortune. The ATR system of morality generally views all human beings as equals. When someone has too much good luck or too many advantages, they upset the moral balance of the world. Success can be explained, therefore, not as someone's greed or desire to gain advantage, but as the result of their consulting a skilled spiritual adviser adept at providing them with spiritual powers responsible for their success. This is one way African belief systems interpret why people flourish or suffer.

The British, Germans, and other Europeans who colonized Africa from the seventeenth to the mid-twentieth century brought with them assumptions about the superiority of their worldview. This included their games, which they determined could be used to inculcate a rational and scientific worldview and "modernize" native cultures. Games that were based on a "clock" would teach time management and organization, for example. They also assumed that modern sports would teach Christian values like teamwork, discipline, and respect for authority. To achieve that goal, they banned ancient African games and rituals. Africans responded by blending their traditions with the newly imported sports including football.[3] Football, due to its similarity to other games that were common in African cultures, ultimately became the most popular sport in Africa. But for Africans to fit football into traditional African culture it had to be infused with their ancient practices, including juju. Aware that juju would conflict with the European worldview Africans hid the rituals from the watchful eye of the colonizers.

In the postcolonial era, independent African nations were often eager to be considered "modern," and juju rituals remained hidden. More and more African players (over a thousand currently) began to play professionally in the premier European leagues, and the Confederation of African Football (CAF) bureaucratized the game. African countries sponsored strong national teams that have qualified for the World Cup and Olympic finals since the 1970s, culminating in the 2010 FIFA World Cup Finals that were held in South Africa. The cultural intermixing led to complications for juju and its practitioners; CAF banned juju outright in 2002, stating explicitly that they did not want African football to suffer from a "third world image." African players, influenced by European standards, reported being embarrassed by juju, claiming it is "sending bad signals about Africa."[4] But the ban is no more effective than those imposed by the colonial rulers in the seventeenth century, and despite protests juju remains a central feature of the African game today in virtually every country in sub-Saharan Africa.[5] Conflicts over juju among players, coaches, politicians, CAF officials, sportswriters, and fans reveal some of the tensions of a global society where differences aren't always respected, even among people who share religious affiliations and national origins.

Juju ceremonies and rituals are surprising to the Western observer. They have two purposes: to imbue players with spiritual power before contests and to protect them from the corresponding power their rivals have gained from their own juju specialists (who cannot work for both sides), often by creating rituals to weaken the other team. Rituals regularly involve animals. Birds are sacrificed and their blood smeared on the players' legs; porcupine and chicken blood are also commonly used in this way. Birds' heads are burned, and their ashes sprinkled on the pitch. Goats have been buried beneath the pitch. Monkey, zebra, and lion bones are rubbed on players to make them run faster, move more deceptively, and be more courageous. Uniforms have been smeared with pork fat for protection. These rituals are sometimes done by a juju man, but the tasks are also delegated to coaches and to the players themselves.

Descriptions of potions that contain salt, ash, herbs, and various oils as well as other unknown substances abound. These are used to wash uniforms and are placed in amulets (also called jujus) hung around the players' necks or sometimes on the goalposts or hidden in shoes. They are rubbed into razor gashes made on players' bodies and faces. In 2005 the president of Gambia reportedly sprinkled a substance from a bottle on the pitch in the Under 17 Africa Cup against Ghana.[6]

More dramatic rituals occasionally involve jumping over bonfires, communing with human corpses, and middle-of-the-night visits to the cemetery to connect with the ancestors. Reports from Tanzania and South Africa describe bringing team members to the bush before dawn on the day of a game to have them climb into termite hills filled with a potion the juju man prepared for them.[7]

Juju specialists use various strategies to analyze how to get an edge for their teams. One Tanzanian juju man was portrayed in the film *Kick the Lion* conversing with the ancestors on a small conch shell; he was communicating with his deceased grandmother who gave him pointers as he picked up her vibrations. Ambani, a Kenyan juju man, divines strategies directly from patterns of small seashells.[8]

Other rituals are designed to foil the opposing team. These include having juju men stand on the sidelines and play drums loudly to cause confusion. Often juju men or players write the names of rival players on eggs or coconuts and smash them. In 2013 the Nigerian coach took a photograph of a Malian man breaking two raw eggs on their side of the field. He ordered the mess cleaned up, but would not tell his players for fear they would worry about the consequences.[9] It was also common practice to light candles and even to urinate on the field to dispel curses, although recently, given the power of virtual reality, a juju man named Mwanachuwoni commented: "We do it by remote control. You write the names of the star players on a tree trunk, cover them up with a black cloth as to blindfold them, and on the match day they will not be seeing the ball."[10]

Placement of jujus (amulets) on the pitch has occasionally led to violence. One famous incident took place in 2003 when Rwanda played Uganda in a qualifying game for the Africa Nations cup. A Ugandan security guard picked up what he believed to be jujus from the Rwandan goalmouth. A fight took place when Ugandan players saw the Rwandan goalkeeper lighting "a mysterious substance" in his goalmouth, which was removed by the Ethiopian official at halftime. The newspaper reported, ironically, that the official "ostentatiously crossed himself before picking it up."[11]

Players also avoid curses by staying away from places that the home team might have protected with ritual objects or ceremonies. They might climb around the stadium rather than entering through the main gate, walk backward onto the pitch, or avoid shaking hands with their opponents. It is common practice to avoid using the dressing rooms if you are the visiting team and not unusual to see teams arrive already in uniform. In one extreme case a few decades ago, the Nigerian team stayed in their country's embassy to avoid sleeping in a hotel in the Cameroons.[12]

Players and teams have begun to speak out against these practices. Sometimes they are accused of betrayal, of doing this to work magic on behalf of the opposing team. In Congo an accusation that a player was using juju sparked a riot that killed thirteen spectators, mostly children, in 2008.[13] Fights within teams over juju have been a concern. In 2011 some members of the Ghanaian national team accused other members of using juju against their own teammates to gain an advantage; the fights were confirmed by Ghana's coach who blamed their loss in the 2012 Africa Cup semifinals to dissension over these accusations, causing team disunity.[14]

Juju men have also been known to curse teams that have failed to pay them after a success. The team from Cote d'Ivoire won the Africa Cup Finals in 1992. The fans and the juju men publicly claimed responsibility for the victory, noting that they had been hired by the Ministry of Sport to accomplish this goal. But they were never paid and put a curse on the national team that won nothing for the subsequent decade. Eventually the ministry apologized and offered the juju men $2,000 to go back to work "for the republic."[15]

How much the juju men are paid has also become an issue. Most national teams have at least one juju specialist on payroll, and some have one for each of their players, a situation that caused the French head coach of the Nigerian team to quit in 1998.[16] Those who dislike the practice claim the money would be better spent on paying the players or for the services of a sports psychologist. But juju men are a big business in African football and clearly are integral to the game.

ACTIVITIES

ACTIVITY 1

Read the following viewpoints that have been articulated about African football and juju:

One

"So I ask, if witchcraft spells are so potent, why is it that an African team has never won the World Cup? Why are many African players not doing well in Europe and America? Is African witchcraft only effective within Africa, within African teams, and among African players playing in Africa? I would ask teams that have fallen out of the current tournament in South Africa: Where is the sting of your juju, charms, magic and muti (potions)? Where are your witchdoctors, spiritualists and marabous (a Muslim religious leader who keeps African traditions)? At the ongoing soccer fiesta in South Africa, the team Burkina Faso has a witch doctor on the grounds. He came with his full magical 'regalia and paraphenalia.'"[17]

Two

"Many European and South American soccer stars, including those currently playing in the World Cup, adhere to strict pregame rituals. England defender John Terry, for example, says he always sits in the same place on the bus traveling to the game. He also must tie the tapes around his socks that hold shin guards in place three times before a game. During this World Cup, Spanish striker Raul Gonzalez was reportedly berated for turning up at practice wearing a yellow T-shirt. His coach, Luis Aragones, considers yellow bad luck. (France went on to knock Spain out of the cup on Tuesday.) Before every game Argentina's former coach Carlos Bilardo used to borrow toothpaste from one of his players. He started the ritual before Argentina's first match in the 1986 World Cup, which his team went on to win. Former Italy coach Giovanni Trappatoni could be seen sprinkling holy water on the playing field from a bottle provided by his sister, a nun."[18]

Three

"This is a very intriguing debate that will never die out, and being the Africans that we are, we must leave with the fact that using juju for whatever purpose is quite a common occurrence our societies, even the Very Important Person(s) are victims of such beliefs. And when it comes to sports, football in particular [in this case, our local footballers], the use of juju is part of their DNA, and no one can pretend to think that they can actually fight it, it's so rampant that it's disgusting to even think of it. I'm not condoning the use of juju to win football matches, but if an individual believes in it and firmly thinks that he can't win without it, what's wrong with that?"[19]

Four

"Defenders of soccer sorcery say that juju men merely psych up players. They are no different from the sport psychologists that many U.S. professional teams maintain on their staff. 'They are throwing out the baby with the bathwater just because some soccer administrators wish to appease the white man more than honor African culture,' one traditional healer from Swaziland responded. 'To depart for an international competition without consulting or including sorcerers is akin to going to an exam without a pencil,' the authoritative African Soccer magazine said in a recent issue.'"[20]

Five

"'Juju does not work at all. Players should just train hard and results will come. People can use a lot of stuff like snuff, but it does not work at all. It is just a question of mind games,' he said with a chuckle. The television presenter was predictably snooty about these 'superstitious' practices, but he should have checked the side altars at Notre Dame before sneering. I surprised six faithful French fans there this week—lighting tapers for Les Bleu."[21]

Order these five quotations from the one you agree with most (#1) to the one you agree with least (#5). Using the information from the case study, provide a one-sentence explanation for your decision about each case. Compare your responses with a partner. Discuss the one quote that you have the widest disagreement about and then describe your partner's point of view. (If you agree about all the quotes, find someone else who does not agree.) When you conclude, find a second pair of students that used the same quote as you for your disagreement. Take turns arguing your partner's position and then your own.

ACTIVITY 2

Go to the *New York Times* database and find the article by John Branch, "Fright Nights in the N. B. A." (April 19, 2014). Imagine you are a juju man (or woman) who is being consulted by an N.B.A. player on their way to Oklahoma City. What advice would you give him and why?

RESOURCES

"Kick the Lion" Dir. Oliver Becker, Occasione Documentaries.

Leseth, Anne. "The Use of Juju in Football: Sport and Witchcraft in Tanzania." In Gary Armstrong and Richard Giulianotti, eds., *Entering the Field: New Perspectives on World Football*, 159–174. Oxford: Berg, 1997.

CASE 6

Jewish Umpires and Baseball Chapel

Fig. 6.1. Josh Miller, Minor League umpire. Courtesy of Josh Miller.

GOAL: To decide if Baseball Chapel should have an official role in professional baseball.

On February 2, 2008, Murray Chass, a *New York Times* sports columnist, wrote an essay entitled, "Should a Clubhouse Be a Chapel?" He was writing in response to a phone call he received from Josh Miller, a minor league umpire who had recently been released by Major League Baseball. Baseball rules require that umpires who are not likely to be promoted to the majors serve no more than three years in AAA ball. While Miller was disappointed, he finally felt free to contact the press about a situation that had disturbed him deeply. Miller felt he could not speak while working in professional baseball for fear that it would have been held against him when his work was being evaluated for promotion.

Miller told Chass that as a Jew he was deeply uncomfortable with Baseball Chapel. Miller explained that Sunday prayer services took place right before the game in the umpires' dressing room. Often the chapel leaders held separate services for the umpires so they wouldn't have to mix with the players. Miller didn't want to be rude, he explained. Often there was no place else to go to do his pregame preparation. Even if he explained that he was Jewish, the preachers would still pray "in Jesus' name." Sometimes other crew members would take offense if he left. "One umpire I worked with last year called me Jewie," he told Chass, "and I said I wasn't comfortable with it. It took a more senior guy to get him to stop."

Miller knew Chass was a sympathetic person to contact because of another incident involving Jews and Baseball Chapel that he had written about. In 2005 Washington Nationals player Ryan Church reported that he asked the volunteer chapel leader, Joe Moeller (who worked professionally as an FBI agent), if his ex-girlfriend, a Jew, was "doomed." Moeller nodded. Church publicly responded: My ex-girlfriend! I was like, man, if they only knew. Other religions don't know any better. It's up to us to spread the word."

Laura Blumenfeld of the *Washington Post* had reported Church's comments as part of an article about Moeller and Baseball Chapel.[1] A local Orthodox rabbi, Shmuel Herzfeld, was deeply offended. He organized a press conference and questioned whether "the locker room of the Nationals is being used to preach hatred." Moeller was relieved of his duties by the Nationals, whose president, Tony Tavares, also apologized on Church's behalf. The written statement said, "Those who know me on a personal level understand that I am not the type of person who would call into question the religious beliefs of others. I sincerely regret if the quote attributed to me in Sunday's *Washington Post* article offended anyone."[2] Neither Moeller nor Baseball Chapel made a public statement, but local Christian clergy acknowledged that Moeller was simply assenting to a standard Christian belief that anyone who doesn't accept Jesus Christ as their savior is putting themselves in jeopardy of eternal damnation.

Following up on the story, the *Washington Post* reported an exchange between Rabbi Ari Sunshine, leader of a Conservative congregation in Olney, Maryland and (Jewish) Baseball Commissioner Bud Selig. Sunshine wrote to Selig asking him to investigate Baseball Chapel and to explain why that organization is "the sole Christian ministry granted access" to all teams. In his letter, Sunshine pointed out that other Christian denominations don't "emphasize 'faith-based' salvation to a degree that denigrates legitimate religious alternatives" and could make for healthier relationships. Sunshine suggested that rotating chaplains of various denominations, as is the practice in some other sports, would better honor religious diversity.[3] The very next day, Sunshine received a reply from Selig agreeing that Moeller's comments were offensive. The commissioner said he would review the relationship with Baseball Chapel, and Major League Baseball spokesman Rich Levin made that promise public.[4]

Three years later Murray Chass reported that Selig had not responded to repeated attempts made by Sunshine and Herzfeld to find out what had happened to the review.[5] Selig did, however respond to Chass in 2008. "'I have to leave that up to each team,' Selig said in an interview. 'If players want to have that type of thing, they're entitled to have them. I frankly think people are free to make that choice.'"[6] While one might assume that as a Jew Selig would have been uncomfortable supporting the exclusive rights of evangelizing Christians, or at least would try to make it easier for a Jewish umpire to function in their midst, that clearly was not the case. Rather, Selig's reaction fit the mold of a liberal American Jew for whom the first amendment's promise of freedom of religion held the highest value. Like many Jews of his generation, Selig believes that freedom of religion is what makes America a safe place for Jews and feels he must uphold that value even when Jews are inconvenienced or made to feel unwelcome. And it would have been difficult for him to challenge the formidable organization known as Baseball Chapel.

Since the 1970s most major professional and collegiate sports teams in the United States have chaplains (including many who are paid for their services), whose roles resemble those of juju men in African football (see case 5). While many of those chaplains are connected to evangelical organizations like Athletes in Action or the Fellowship of Christian Athletes, they may also be Catholic, liberal Protestant, Jewish, or Muslim. But the relationship of Baseball Chapel to professional baseball is unique.

Beginning in the 1960s, teams like the Minnesota Twins and Chicago Cubs, in response to players who missed the opportunity to go to church before Sunday afternoon games on the road, held religious services for their players at their hotels. At that time, baseball clubhouses were dominated by players for whom drinking, cursing, and staying out late was the norm, and religious Christians found themselves in the minority and uncomfortable with the general atmosphere where they were sometimes teased about their beliefs. For example, two New York Yankees, Bobby Richardson and Tony Kubek, were often called the "milkshake boys" by their notoriously wild teammates. But in the 1970s a cultural shift occurred. With the help of broadcaster Red Barber, Kubek and Richardson organized Sunday prayer services for the Yankees, too.

Seizing the moment, Watson (Waddy) Spoelstra (1910–1999) made a bold move. In 1973 Spoelstra (grandfather of Miami Heat basketball coach Eric) retired as a sportswriter with the *Detroit News* to devote his life to creating Baseball Chapel. He had not always been a religious man. In his earlier life he had been a heavy drinker. His conversion came in 1957 when his daughter miraculously recovered from a brain hemorrhage–

induced coma. In gratitude, Spoelstra decided to dedicate his life to God. He continued his sports writing career, serving as president of the Baseball Writers Association of America in 1968, but became more and more immersed in religious life at the same time. He quit drinking and became active in his church.

He was open about his faith, but his interests in religion and baseball never came together until the 1970s, when Spoelstra and Detroit Tigers announcer Ernie Harwell organized Sunday services for Tigers players in hotel rooms when they were on the road, modeled on the example set by the Yankees, Cubs, and Twins. Inspired to take the plan further, Spoelstra approached Bowie Kuhn, the baseball commissioner and a devout Roman Catholic, with his idea for what Spoelstra called Baseball Chapel. Kuhn gave Spoelstra official permission and $5,000. Spoelstra went into action. Within three years all 26 major league teams had Baseball Chapel, and by 1978 there was a program for every minor league team as well. Today they serve the 210 major league teams and their minor league affiliates, Latin American winter leagues, and many independent teams as well.[7]

It was Spoelstra's idea to move the services from the hotel to the ballpark where players would be more relaxed. The move also increased access and interest. He found local volunteers (often but not necessarily clergy) to coordinate and lead. The services were brief—fifteen to twenty minutes. Leaders introduce short prayers and give an inspirational homily. Bible reading is not included in the typical prayer service, but Bible study sessions were added later based on interest. Each team also had a player representative to coordinate with local Baseball Chapel volunteers in other cities. Spoelstra recruited future Hall of Famers like Hank Aaron and Reggie Jackson for the jobs. These prestigious players secured the reputation of Baseball Chapel. On most teams at least half the players began to attend regularly, and sometimes even a higher percentage of players are involved.

The organization continued to grow and develop. In 1982 Bowie Kuhn recognized Spoelstra's contributions to baseball with the prestigious Commissioner's Trophy. Spoelstra served as president until 1983. Bobby Richardson, former New York Yankee second baseman, followed him in that role, serving from 1984–1994. Richardson made closer connections between the organization and Athletes in Action. As a former player, he also increased the legitimacy of Baseball Chapel. In 1995 Vince Nauss took over as president. Nauss, a licensed minister, also has a degree in sports management. He worked for Major League Baseball under Bowie Kuhn, and as publicity director for the Philadelphia Phillies. Baseball Chapel has six full-time staff. Given the percentage of players of Latino ancestry in baseball, two staff members devote themselves to Latino Ministries in the U.S. and Latin America. Two staff members are assigned to develop and train chaplains. Part-time staff members work on the ministries to umpires and two female staff members are assigned to work with players' wives. Although attendance began to taper off in the twenty-first century, the Web site claims that they still serve approximately three thousand baseball personnel every year. With the exception of the Colorado Rockies, who have hired their own professional chaplain, Baseball Chapel is the only religious institution officially affiliated with professional baseball.

Many of the players who come are already devout, while others discover their devotion through attendance. Wives, coaches, managers and staff are welcomed, and separate services are conducted for the visiting team and umpires. The services provide players with fellowship, team cohesion, and a quiet time to focus and reflect before games. Services are informal, and the leader usually gives an inspirational message that ties Christian values to playing the game. They do not ever claim that prayers are efficacious for winning ball games or hitting home runs, however. The weekly routine is particularly helpful to minor league players who are young and open to distraction. The game of baseball is humbling; these encounters with religious teachings help players deal with adversity. Many teams provide a clubhouse room for the event. But, particularly in minor league parks, space is tighter, and meetings can take place in a corner of the stands, in hallways, and in dressing rooms.

Baseball Chapel provides support for the approximately five hundred volunteer chaplains in the form of weekly sermon topics and a calendar of Bible verses suitable for homilies in Spanish and English. Chaplains are responsible for recruiting players and other personnel to attend. Every player and umpire receives a handout with the official Baseball Chapel logo inviting them to participate.[8]

Baseball Chapel has a complex relationship with the media. Media representatives are not allowed to attend services, and services are never recorded. Although the Web site states that team chapel leaders may not grant interviews, a search on the Web will reveal dozens of feature articles about them (including Laura Blumenfeld's *Washington Post* conversation with Joe Moeller). Despite the strict confidentiality, many players want to talk openly about their faith. Several have written books, and there are dozens of video testimonials on the Baseball Chapel Web site. The Web site banner features recent stars R. A. Dickey and Josh Hamilton, both of whom have written extensively about faith.

Of course, not everyone was pleased with the institutionalization of Sunday prayer in baseball. Some managers thought that having some players go and others refrain would be a divisive influence. A serious and public disagreement between born-again Minnesota Twin Gary Gaetti and his former friend Kent Hrbek hurt team chemistry in 1988.[9] In other instances managers reported resenting the time taken away from pregame preparation. The father of one minor leaguer complained that his Jewish son was being ostracized as he had to sit outside the locker room during prayers.[10]

Some critics, like the rabbis we discussed, have expressed concern that Baseball Chapel is exclusively evangelical and has a clear mission to proselytize. Their Web site lists the mission: "To bring encouragement to people in the world of professional baseball through the Gospel so that some become discipled followers of Jesus Christ." Their statement of faith asserts that they believe the Old and New Testaments to be the "infallible Word of God" that reveals God's will. God is triune and "eternally exists in three Persons—Father, Son and Holy Spirit." Jesus Christ "became flesh and dwelt among us as both fully God and fully man, was born of a virgin the only Son of the Father. He lived a sinless life, was obedient to the Father, allowing Himself to be crucified as the only substitution for our sins, died and rose again on the third day, ascended into heaven and will visibly, bodily return again in judgment and in blessing to reign forever."

Their doctrine is, as Rabbi Sunshine and Murray Chass lamented, exclusivist, denying anyone who is not Christian access to heaven. Baseball Chapel does support the doctrine that claims: "Sinful people may be reconciled to God only through the shed blood of Jesus Christ, who conquered death in resurrection and offers eternal life to all who believe and receive. This salvation is not through works, but by grace alone through faith in Christ." Those who do not believe are subject to "everlasting punishment separated from God."[11]

ACTIVITIES

ACTIVITY 1

Research project

Investigate the history of Christian efforts to convert Jews in the United States and decide whether Baseball Chapel should be understood in this light or not.

ACTIVITY 2

Role play

Form groups of five. Each group will consist of someone playing the role of Bud Selig, Vince Nauss, Rabbi Ari Sunshine, and Murray Chass. The fifth group member will serve in the capacity of group moderator. In this scenario the actors will sit down together and discuss possible resolutions to the problems experienced by umpire Joshua Miller. Research what position each actor would take.

Consider the following questions:

Who should have the authority to make decision?
Should MLB officially sanction Baseball Chapel?
Should there be a separation of religion and baseball?
Should the media play a role at all?

Does Baseball Chapel, which allows Christians to join voluntarily for worship in their workplace, invade the rights of others?

RESOURCES

Kashatus, William C. "The Origins of Baseball Chapel and the Era of the Christian Athlete, 1973–1990." *Nine: A Journal of Baseball History and Social Policy Perspectives* 7.2 (Spring 1999): 75–90.

Krattenmaker, Tom. "Church at the Ballpark." In *Onward Christian Athletes: Turning Ballparks Into Pulpits and Players Into Preachers,* 87–106. Lanham, MD: Rowman and Littlefield, 2010.

Price, Joseph L. *Rounding the Bases: Baseball and Religion in America,* 29–36. Macon, GA: Mercer University Press, 2006.

PART 3

WHAT HAPPENS WHEN RELIGION AND SPORTS COME INTO CONFLICT?

These cases will illustrate what happens when sports are the arena in which athletes test their religious values and beliefs. In case 7 we look at the famous Nazi Olympics that took place in Berlin in 1936. As many people and governments began to fear the goals of Nazi Germany, they wondered if they should boycott the Olympics. The United States decided to participate over the objections of Jewish and other groups who pressed a boycott. We will ask if American Jewish athletes should have participated in the 1936 Berlin Olympics. Does participation make a better form of protest than boycott when values collide? Case 8 also comes from that era and illustrates the problem that arises when religious practices and sports priorities conflict. The case you will study in this context is about a black Jewish baseball team (the Belleville Grays) that refused to compete on Saturdays in the Negro Leagues. The conflicts the Grays experienced were not only about religious observance but also about the economic practices in the world of semiprofessional baseball and so make for a most interesting story of the conflict between religion and sports. Case 9 focuses on Mahmoud Abdul-Rauf, a basketball player for the Denver Nuggets in the 1990s, who refused to stand for the National Anthem based on his interpretation of Muslim values.

Abdul-Rauf contended that being compelled to participate was in conflict with the beliefs of Islam as he interprets them. Although the case was settled amicably through negotiation, fans responded by targeting a local mosque, and Abdul-Rauf's career trajectory changed radically; a particularly painful conflict between religion and sports. Case 10 surfaces questions about how comfortable we are with accommodating public displays of religion in sports as well as the importance of taking gender into account in these conflicts. Here we tell the story of Wojdan Ali Seraj Abdulrahim Shahrkhani who was allowed to compete in the judo matches in the 2012 Olympics as one of two women representing Saudi Arabia—the last country to permit women's Olympic participation. The conflict, however, was not with Saudi participation, but rather the fact that Wojdan would only compete if she was allowed to wear hijab (a specially designed headscarf that met judo federation criteria).

CASE 7

American Jews and the Boycott of the 1936 Berlin Olympics

Fig. 7.1. A pedestrian reads a notice announcing an upcoming public meeting, scheduled for Tuesday, December 3, 1935, at the Mecca Temple in New York City, to urge Americans to boycott the 1936 Berlin Olympics. United States Holocaust Memorial Museum, courtesy of National Archives and Records Administration, College Park.

GOAL: Decide whether if you were an American Jewish athlete you would have boycotted the 1936 Olympics in Berlin.

The modern-day Olympics came to be because of the passion of one man—Pierre de Coubertin, a French aristocrat and educator. In 1896 he realized his dream to have athletes in different sports come together to compete on behalf of their nations in a spirit of fair play and open competition. To Coubertin these games would foster international goodwill and serve as an antidote to international strife. These noble goals were soon complicated by the march toward war in Europe. In 1916 the games were supposed to be held in Germany, but they were canceled due to the outbreak of the First World War. As punishment for their role in the war, Germany was banned from participating in the two subsequent games held in 1920 and 1924. But the International Olympic Committee lifted the ban in 1928 and in 1931 decided that the 1936 games should be held in Germany to make amends for past ill will.

In January 1933 the National Socialists (Nazi) became the ruling party in Germany. The Chancellor, Adolf Hitler, was initially disinterested in hosting this international sporting event, claiming it was alien to the German spirit. But Hitler was slowly convinced by his minister of propaganda, Joseph Goebbels, that the Olympics would be a good opportunity to show off the "New Germany" to an international audience.

By April the Nazis had begun a campaign against the Jewish population of Germany that included a one-day boycott of Jewish goods and services; the elimination of Jews from professions such as teaching, medicine, the law, and civil service; and barring Jews from membership in sports organizations. This had an immediate impact on one of the men who was working to bring the Olympics to Germany, Theodor Lewald. Lewald served on the International Olympic Committee (IOC) and as president of the German Olympic Committee (GOC). He was also the head of the ministry of sport and taught at the German sport university. He was removed from the positions in Germany because of his Jewish ancestry—Lewald's maternal grandfather had been a convert to Christianity many years before, but one (biological) Jewish grandparent made Lewald a Jew by German racial standards.

Jewish athletes in Germany were also affected by these laws. Gretel Bergmann, a Jewish high jumper and potential Olympic qualifier, was dropped by the sports organization where she trained, the Ulm Football Club. Gretel's parents sent her to England, along with other Jewish athletes who had the means to leave an environment that was becoming increasingly hostile.

As conditions changed in Germany, international concerns rose. The *Baltimore Jewish Times* suggested the 1936 Olympic Games should be moved from Germany as part of larger cultural and economic boycott effort. The protest was soon joined by the American Jewish Congress. The head of the American Olympic Committee (AOC), Avery Brundage, agreed that it was important for the IOC to look into the matter, "equality of the races" being a key Olympic ideal.

Despite outside pressure, the new Reich sports commissioner, Hans von Tschammer und Osten, refused to make concessions, insisting that German sports were for Aryans and only Aryans would represent the nation. But the Nazis were willing to concede that all foreign nationals entering the country to compete would be treated with hospitality.

The International Olympic Committee took up the question of Germany's failure to comply with Olympic ideals at their meeting in Vienna in June. The IOC president, Belgian Henri Baillet Latour, was committed to the idea that the Olympics should remain above politics. He worried about Nazi interference with the IOC's ability to exercise control over the games. After long discussions, the IOC laid down several conditions. Theodor Lewald was to be retained as head of the GOC, all Olympic customs were to be observed, and German Jews could not be excluded from German teams.

The Nazis assured the IOC that they would comply, and Latour took them at their word. The Germans did follow the letter, but not the spirit, of the requirements. As American consul general George Messersmith reported in correspondence with the U.S. State Department, Lewald remained head of the GOC, but in name only. German Jews were granted the nominal right to compete, but the conditions that existed (excluding Jews from private clubs and sports organizations while requiring membership in those clubs to qualify for Olympic trials) would make it impossible for them to train or prepare adequately.

The IOC was satisfied with Germany's nominal compliance. But American Jewish groups who doubted the Nazis would keep their word pressed the issue of a possible United States boycott of the Berlin Olympics, knowing that if the United States refused to participate then Britain and France would also likely withdraw and the Olympic Games would effectively be canceled. Led by Bernard Deutsch and Rabbi Stephen Wise of the American Jewish Congress and Samuel Untermeyer of the Non-Sectarian Anti-Nazi League, they called upon universities and the Amateur Athletic Union (AAU), the organization that had the power to determine athletes' amateur status and thus their eligibility to participate in the Olympics, to use their influence to keep the United States from participating. Both the AAU and the AOC took up the question of whether the U.S. should boycott the Olympics at their meetings in November.

American sports leaders had mixed reactions. Charles Orenstein and Gus Kirby, AOC members, thought the U.S. should boycott unless there was real evidence that German Jews would have opportunities to train and practice. George Sherrill, one of three U.S. representatives to the IOC, argued that a boycott would only increase antisemitism because American athletes would blame Jews if they couldn't compete and a boycott would do nothing to help the Jews of Germany. Others pointed out that in the United States both African Americans and Jews were discriminated against in sports. For example, Jews were not allowed in a restricted club that was to host the 1932 Winter Games in Lake Placid, New York. And boxing and track events often had to relocate from the South where blacks were not allowed to compete. Statements encouraging the German government to make sure Jews would be able to train were issued by both groups (the AAU statement somewhat stronger than the AOC's), but no final decision was made.

In January 1934 the Germans sent out invitations to the Eleventh Olympiad. The AOC decided that before accepting the invitation they would send the president, Avery Brundage, to Germany that summer to investigate. The U.S. boycott movement staged a mass rally in the spring that indicated both numerical strength and broadened participation, including leaders from labor and government.

In September Brundage reported that all conditions in Germany were favorable. He claimed to have met with Jewish sports leaders, all of whom were satisfied with their treatment. His trip was planned by IOC and GOC member Karl Ritter Von Halt, who determined which athletes Brundage met and also provided translation for him. Brundage observed that in the United States private clubs like the one he belonged to in Chicago also excluded Jews, and the current U.S. legal standard of "separate but equal" applied in both cases. The AOC vote based on Brundage's report was a unanimous decision to participate, although one member, Charles Orenstein, still expressed his disapproval. George Sherrill, member of the IOC, corroborated that the Nazis had invited seventeen Jews to train and that two Jewish clubs were asked to submit more names.

The boycott movement also grew in strength, supported by New York political leaders: Congressman Emanuel Celler, the popular Mayor Fiorello LaGuardia, and Governor Al Smith. And George Messersmith, now serving as ambassador to Austria, again recommended to the State Department that the U.S. boycott the games. He pointed out that all German sport was now controlled by the government. He presumed that their goal was to train Nazi youth, evidenced by the fact that even Catholic and Protestant youth groups were no longer allowed to function independent of Nazi control. Finally, Messersmith concluded that the Nazis would attempt to use the Olympics to enhance their international standing. President Roosevelt was silent on the subject of U.S. participation and would remain so.

In 1935, a Gallup Poll indicated that 43 percent of Americans agreed that the United States should refuse to participate in Olympics held in Berlin. The release of the poll coincided with anti-Jewish riots in Berlin and an increase in virulent racist graffiti in Munich. The boycott movement grew beyond the Jewish community to include organizations such as the Catholic War Veterans, the two leading Christian journals (*Christian Century* and *Commonweal*), prominent liberal Protestant clergy Reinhold

Niebuhr and Harry Emerson Fosdick, and arch Catholic antisemite Father Charles Coughlin. It was endorsed by the *New York Times* and several African American newspapers. The movement also included a powerful sports leader, the new president of the AAU, Jeremiah Mahoney, who was deeply distressed by anti-Jewish violence.

Meanwhile, Avery Brundage made public statements defending U.S. participation. He noted the lack of past Jewish athletic participation in the Olympics, suggesting the Nazi policies affected very few individuals. He argued that the Olympics must be free from any "racial, religious, or political" concerns. Like the leaders of the IOC, Brundage's main concern was that the Olympics go on.

In September, the Nazis promulgated the Nuremberg Laws. Under this new legislation, anyone with one Jewish grandparent was no longer to be counted as a German citizen. From then on Jews had no political rights. Sex and marriage between Jews and Aryans were also outlawed. Jews could not retain Aryans as domestic servants and were prohibited from flying the Nazi flag.

Sensing an opportunity, George Sherrill of the IOC demanded that the Germans comply with their promise of allowing Jews on the German Olympic teams. The German response was to invite two athletes to train for the Olympic Games. High jumper Gretel Bergmann was recalled from England and fencer Helene Mayer was asked to return from the United States. Mayer, whose father was Jewish, but was neither raised nor identified as a Jew, was happy to return. Bergmann, whose family had remained in Germany, worried that they would be harmed if she did not comply. Another half-Jewish hockey player, Rudi Ball, was also asked to return from Switzerland to play in the upcoming Winter Games, held in Garmisch-Partenkirchen.

Thereafter Sherrill considered the matter closed, declaring, "I would have no more business discussing that in Germany than if the Germans attempted to discuss the Negro situation in the American South or the treatment of Japanese in California."[1] The AOC published a pamphlet, *Fair Play for American Athletes*, denouncing the boycott. They deemed it a threat to amateur sports and asserted that American athletes should not be forced to be martyrs. The Olympics, they again suggested, should be free of politics and not get involved in what was termed the "present Jew-Nazi altercation." City College president Frederick Robinson came out against the boycott, arguing that it would be better for the U.S. to send a strong team that included Jews and display the power of living in a diverse and open society.

But AAU president Jeremiah Mahoney did his own investigation and came to the conclusion that the Nazis were themselves politicizing sports by using it as part of their discriminatory practices. He called for Theodor Lewald to resign and reiterated the argument that Jewish athletes could not possibly be getting proper training given the conditions under which they were living, especially since most of them were already either in exile or had committed suicide. The newly organized Committee on Fair Play reiterated Mahoney's contentions in a pamphlet that listed over forty Nazi edicts that discriminated against Jewish participation in sports.

Although one of the other American members of the IOC, William Garland, agreed with Sherrill, the other member, Ernst Lee Jahncke, who himself had German ancestry, did not. Jahncke wrote an open letter to IOC president Latour suggesting that the games should be withdrawn from Berlin, characterizing Nazi policies and ideology as inimical to the Olympic ideals of fair play. He also rejected the notion that the U.S. had no right to speak because of its own history of discrimination, differentiating between private and state-sponsored racism.

In December the boycott movement held another mass meeting, and forty-one college presidents signed a public petition in favor of the boycott, arguing that the Nazis were using the games to push forward their discriminatory agenda. Walter White, head of the NAACP, also joined the boycott movement. The African American community was divided on the subject. Some noted that it would be important for America to see black athletes triumph. Black athletes themselves pointed out that they were treated better in Germany than in the American South and that even in the North they were denied equal housing and opportunities to participate in sports, including in the segregated national pastime, baseball. Others disagreed, supporting the notion that discrimination should be fought wherever it took place.

Later that month, the AAU took a vote that called for individual athletes to boycott, for the AOC to rescind its approval, for the IOC to change the venue, and for their own further investigation of Nazi policies to continue. The vote was purely symbolic, as the AAU had no power to enact those changes. The motion was ultimately defeated, albeit by a narrow margin, 58.25 to 55.75. German newspapers reported the result as an affirmation, omitting to mention the close vote tally.

As a result, the pro-boycott leaders at the IOC and AOC, Ernst Jahncke and Charles Orenstein, were forced out of their respective positions, and Jeremiah Mahoney resigned as president of the AAU, to be replaced by Avery Brundage. Brundage would remain the single most powerful American Olympic official through the 1972 Olympics in Munich.

As 1936 approached, Germany prepared for the games. Joseph Goebbels announced that the entire event would be made into a major motion picture by Leni Riefenstahl to publicize the "new Germany" far and wide. Jewish persecution would be temporarily abandoned, anti-Jewish signs and graffiti would be removed, and the Nazis would be on their best behavior. Helene Mayer would be the only "Jew" on the German team. Gretel Bergmann was informed in June by German authorities that she had "underachieved" and did not make the team despite the fact that she was forced to train in segregated facilities, won the Wurttemberg Championship in 1935, and equaled the European high jump mark of 1.6 meters in practice events. (Bergmann was permitted to emigrate to the United States in 1937. She won championships in 1937 and 1938.)

American Jewish athletes faced a choice about whether or not to boycott. Among those who decided not to go to Berlin were track and field qualifiers Milton Green and Norman Cahners. They were persuaded by their rabbi, Harry Levy, not to participate. Herman Neugass, who had tied the world record for the 100 yard run, also declined. They were joined in protest by 1932 Olympic gold medal discus thrower Lillian Copeland, featherweight boxer Louis Gevinson, and the entire Long Island University basketball team composed of four Jews (Jules Bender, Benjamin Kramer, Leo Merson, and William Schwartz) and several Italian and Irish Americans who supported them, including future New York Yankee pitcher Marius Russo. Others participated in a Jewish Olympiad

"World Athletic Carnival" in New York that summer instead; still others contented themselves with participating in the Zionist-sponsored Maccabiah Games in Palestine in 1935.

There were six Jewish athletes who decided to go to Berlin. Herman Goldberg, who was on the Olympic baseball team, wanted to introduce Germans to the sport he loved. Basketball player Sam Balter wanted to see what was going on in Germany for himself. Featherweight lifter Dave Mayor and pistol expert Morris Doob also participated. Not everyone was even aware there was a boycott.

The best-known athletes who decided to show what Jews could do athletically were Marty Glickman and Sam Stoller, who made the track and field team as members of the 4x100 relay race. But they never got to run. The two Jews were replaced the day before the race by African American standouts Ralph Metcalfe and Jesse Owens. This would be Owens's chance for a fourth Olympic medal. He had already proven that he was the fastest man in the world, and he made a powerful example to illustrate the absurdity of Hitler's beliefs in Aryan domination, although Germany did win the most medals at the games.

The day prior to the event, the coaches called a team meeting to inform them that Metcalfe and Owens would replace Glickman and Stoller, suggesting that the German team was stronger than expected and the Americans would need their best to win. After the Americans won easily, it was clear that the threat was exaggerated and not the real reason for the replacement. Did Brundage not want to embarrass Hitler any further—it was bad enough that blacks had been so dominant, how much worse if Jews also stood on the medal stand. Did Owens want a fourth Olympic medal? Were Stoller and Glickman really not the best suited to run the race? We will never know.

ACTIVITIES

ACTIVITY 1A

It is 1936. You are a Jewish athlete and you have been invited onto the U.S. Olympic team. You are looking forward to participating in the 1936

U.S. Olympics in Berlin. Your rabbi, upset at the failure of an American boycott, has pointed out to you that some individual Jewish athletes are refusing to participate in the Olympics, and he asks you to consider staying home. You decide that this is an important issue and you give it serious study and consideration. When you have made up your mind, you write him a letter in reply. In your answer you include specific references to at least four actions taken or ideas expressed (by the German government, the American Olympic Committee, boycott leaders, other athletes, religious traditions) that you found most persuasive in coming to your decision and mention the names of the people whose ideas and actions helped you decide. You also make reference to at least two ideas or actions that do not support your viewpoint and explain why these ideas or actions were not persuasive. You should also speculate about what your decision will mean for you as a Jew and an athlete.

Word limit: 500. Note: Your essay will not be judged based on the decision you made, but on how you make your argument and the sources you choose to back up your decision.

ACTIVITY 1B

In 1972 a local Jewish newspaper asks you to write on how you feel about the decision you made so many years before. Knowing of the experiences of Jesse Owens and Marty Glickman, and the changes in the situation of the Jews in Hitler's Germany that took place after 1936, do you think you made the right decision? Reflect for the newspaper on how you imagine your decision would have affected your life as a Jew and an athlete. How did the experience affect your current view on the relationship of sports to religion and politics? Word limit: 250.

ACTIVITY 2

It is 2008. You are the grandchild of one of the Jewish athletes who decided to boycott the 1936 Olympics. You receive a request to sign the following petition from the David S. Wyman Institute for Holocaust Studies:

August 8, 2008

Hon. Zhou Wenzhong
Office of the Ambassador
Embassy of the People's Republic of China
Washington, D.C.
via email: chinaembassy_us@fmprc.gov.cn
and fax 202–588–9760

Dear Mr. Ambassador:

As the families of American athletes and others who protested against the 1936 Olympics in Nazi Germany because of the persecution of German Jews, we are deeply disappointed that China has revoked the visa of Olympic gold medalist Joey Cheek, who has been critical of China's support for the genocidal government of Sudan.

The lesson our family members taught us is that the Olympics present an opportunity to promote greater international tolerance and understanding. In 2001, China was awarded the right to host this year's Olympics in part because of its promise to permit open access to the games by the international media and to allow those who disagree with Chinese government policies to express themselves. Barring Joey Cheek contravenes the spirit of openness and tolerance that China pledged to facilitate and our family members valued so highly.

Like our parents, Joey Cheek and his colleagues at Team Darfur have spoken out against injustice and oppression. They have a moral right to do so. We respectfully urge your government, in keeping with the Olympic spirit, to restore Mr. Cheek's visa.

Sincerely,[2]

Would you sign this petition? Encourage other members of your family to do so? In your reply to the sponsors of the petition, be sure to give a strong explanation for your decision to sign or not. Do you see a link between the events? Is this a good way to use your connection to your ancestor?

RESOURCES

Gottlieb, Moshe. "The American Controversy Over the Olympic Games." *American Jewish Historical Quarterly* 61.3 (March 1972) 181–213.

Guttmann, Allen, Heather Kestner, and George Eisen. "Jewish Athletes and the Nazi Olympics." In Kay Schaffer and Sidonie Smith, eds., *The Olympics at the Millennium: Power, Politics and the Games,* 51–62. New Brunswick: Rutgers University Press, 2000.

Hilton, Christopher. *Hitler's Olympics: The 1936 Olympic Games.* Stroud: Sutton, 2006.

Large, David Clay. *Nazi Games: The Olympics of 1936,* 69–109, 295–315. New York: Norton, 2007.

Mayer, Paul Yogi. *Jews and the Olympic Games,* 73–132. London: Vallentine Mitchell, 2004.

Taylor, Paul. *Jews and the Olympic Games: The Clash Between Sport and Politics,* 88–92, 250. Brighton: Sussex Academic, 2004.

Walters, Guy. *Berlin Games: How the Nazis Stole the Olympic Dream.* New York: William Morrow, 2006.

View the online exhibition from the US Holocaust Memorial Museum, http://www.ushmm.org/museum/exhibit/online/olympics/, and the podcast of an interview with Susan Bachrach, http://www.ushmm.org /genocide/analysis/details.php?content=2007–02–08.

CASE 8

The Belleville Grays and Playing Sports on the Sabbath

Fig. 8.1. Belleville Grays practice at their home field c. 1920. Courtesy of Joel Wagner

GOAL: To decide whether H. Z. Plummer made appropriate decisions about the role of baseball in his religious community

BACKGROUND

While doing research for *Out of Left Field: Jews and Black Baseball*, I had the opportunity to meet Rabbi Curtis Caldwell from Newark, New Jersey (of blessed memory), who, having heard about my project, wanted to introduce me to a team of black Jews who played against Negro League teams. Before I met him, I had no idea that black Jews played in the Negro Leagues. My study was about the white Jews who owned the teams and also those who fought for baseball's integration. Rabbi Caldwell, sensing my ignorance, brought me a copy of the history of the Church of God and Saints of Christ (COGASOC), also known as Temple Beth El, an international community of Hebrew Israelites with headquarters just outside of Portsmouth, Virginia. He opened the book to a photograph of the communal team, the Belleville Grays, and my odyssey with this story began. With Rabbi Caldwell's help I was able to learn quite a bit about how baseball was used in this Southern religious community to build communal spirit and as a positive investment that would bring outside respect to the community, make an economic contribution to the Tidewater Virginia region, and bring credit to the African American race. Like Eastern European Jews who learned about baseball in order to become American, black Jews saw baseball as way of belonging to America. But for them, belonging meant being welcome only in the segregated world that black baseball embodied while navigating their role as an atypical religious community in the South. What I learned from my study of this group's involvement in Negro League baseball also highlighted the conflicts between their religious commitments and the economics of sport, and that is the focus of this case study.

Rabbi Caldwell, the group's historian, explained to me that the team was the brainchild of the group's charismatic leader, William Plummer, in the early 1920s. Plummer died in 1931 and his son, Howard Zebulon Plummer (1899–1975), became the community's leader and the manager of the baseball team for which he had played second base in his youth. H. Z. Plummer, generally referred to as Bishop Plummer in the black press and as Grandfather Abraham in his own community, had different goals from his father. He wanted to professionalize the team. Although not an official part of the Negro "major" leagues, under Plummer's leadership the Belleville Grays were part of two lesser-known leagues (the Negro International/Colored Eastern League in 1939 and the Interstate League in 1940). They also played independently against local and Negro National and American League teams from the 1920s through the 1950s.[1]

It is not surprising that there is little known about African American Jews whose traditions arose out of the period of enslavement. As a survival technique, blacks concealed much from white society during slavery, and emancipation did little to alter the necessity to continue that path. The archetype of the trickster derived from African myth would reinforce the awareness that guile and deception, mixed with humor, would be useful survival tools in a racist society. What leading black thinker W. E. B. DuBois termed "double consciousness" would help blacks manage the intrusive gaze of the white world. Because so little is known about them, a brief introduction to the group and its historic antecedents is necessary.

What we do know of slave religion in the American South was that it successfully incorporated elements of African traditions (including Jewish, Christian, Muslim and indigenous customs) and mixed them with the version of Protestant Christianity that was taught by the slave masters. This new religious system was based mostly on Hebrew Bible references to liberation from slavery and the images of the chosen people. Preferred Bible passages were those that highlighted the story of the Exodus, the hopes of the Psalms, and the redemption of the book of Revelation. Slaves prayed to a God who delivered Moses, David, and Daniel and were decidedly disinterested in the life and story of Jesus. Psalm 68:31, that "nobles will come out of Egypt and Ethiopia shall stretch her hand towards God" encapsulated hope and also legitimacy of their African heritage.[2]

TEMPLE BETH EL'S JEWISH IDENTITY

Slave religion influenced the thought of William Saunders Crowdy (1847–1908), the founder of COGASOC and William Plummer's teacher and predecessor. Crowdy was the first to take the metaphoric association with Israel literally. African American religious historian Albert Raboteau calls COGASOC a "heterodox" version of Judaism that was one of many efforts to solve the dilemma of racist Christianity. Crowdy founded his movement in 1896. A son of former slaves and a former sharecropper who was living in Texas and working as a cook on the Santa Fe railroad, Crowdy experienced a vision from God that the Negro race was descended from the ten lost tribes of Israel. He quit his job and moved to Lawrence, Kansas, where he founded his church. By 1901 he had moved his headquarters to Philadelphia. In the 1906 census of religious organizations, COGASOC reported 48 organized groups in 14 states with 1,823 members and 75 ministers. Their basic doctrine combined Jewish and Christian teachings and practice. The group followed the Jewish calendar, using Hebrew names for the months and observing Jewish holy days, particularly Passover, the New Year, and a Friday and Saturday sundown-to-sundown Sabbath. They took these holidays seriously, abstaining from any work, particularly on the Sabbath. They also followed standard Baptist practices, confessing faith in Christ, foot washing, and tithing. They engaged more extreme holiness practices such as abstinence from wine and profanity, endogamous marriage, censorship of printed matter and the holy kiss, for which Crowdy got into much trouble.[3]

William Crowdy's following grew. The 1916 census reported ninety-four organized groups with thirty-seven buildings (there was only one building in 1906). By 1936 the community consisted of 213 groups, 79 buildings, and 37,084 members. They also reported groups in the West Indies and an evangelical presence in Africa. In addition to Philadelphia, the group had a major center in Plainfield, New Jersey, and, in 1903, purchased a plot of land near Portsmouth, Virginia, which they called Belleville and which became their international headquarters in 1920. The leader whom Crowdy appointed as one of his successors, William H. Plummer (1868–1931), developed Belleville.

Belleville was the community's "Canaan land," and a remarkable accomplishment. In rural Virginia in the 1920s, Plummer's several-hundred-acre development ran on its own electricity. It housed a sawmill, a building for religious services, a communal dining hall, a music hall, a barbershop, a laundry, a printing plant, an auto repair, blacksmith and carpentry shops, and dormitories for the Belleville Industrial School, which ran from kindergarten through high school and conducted industrial, farming, and religious training. To sustain itself, the community produced lumber for sale and did poultry and dairy farming, along with producing crops of wheat, corn, and peaches. And Plummer also built a wooden baseball stadium on the land. While the rest of the facilities were for community members only, the school (and later a widow and orphans home) and baseball field were open to the public.[4]

RELIGIOUS OBSERVANCE

After Crowdy's death, there was a split in the group as some adherents moved closer to Christian practices while others focused primarily on the Jewish dimensions of Crowdy's teachings. William Plummer led the group that gravitated towards Jewish observances and called themselves Temple Beth El. They proclaimed that they adhered to the religion *of* Jesus, not *about* Jesus, although not all the Christian elements were eliminated from the practice of this group. Their English prayers are adapted from the old Reform *Union Prayer Book*, although they incorporated readings from Christian Scripture, especially the book of Revelation. They also maintained their own versions of Jewish practices. Men and women sit separately. They perform a Torah service although they do not read from the Torah or remove it from the Ark; the scroll is treated like a venerated object. Until the 1950s their Passover celebration incorporated the sacrifice and communal eating of a lamb as described in the book of Exodus. The Passover meal, eaten at midnight in public ritual, was often compared in newspaper accounts to a reenactment of the Last Supper. Quite a few of the Temple Beth El congregations have adopted more traditional Jewish practice, including holiday and life cycle celebrations. Some members of Temple Beth El communities today refer to themselves as Jewish, but others still call themselves Hebrews or Israelites. Although that terminology was originally adopted from American Jews who often referred to themselves in similar terms in the nineteenth century, today it serves to differentiate them from the Ashkenazi Jewish world.[5]

Perhaps the clearest expression of their theology is found in the history the Belleville community put together, where they assert that Crowdy "saw God as integrated and interwoven with all of life (immanent and transcendent)." Blacks needed to recapture the concept of corporate salvation and peoplehood of the Old Testament and move away from Christian individualist doctrine. Since the 1940s their leaders have been called either rabbis or elders. Similar shifts toward Ashkenazi Jewish practices took place in other black Hebrew groups beginning in this era and were primarily influenced by contacts with other Israelite communities, American Ashkenazi Jews, and with Ethiopia and their Jewish community, Beta Israel.

BASEBALL AND RELIGIOUS PRACTICE

By the early 1920s, William Plummer's team of black Jews from Temple Beth El was playing organized baseball against local teams in Virginia. Plummer's vision of a healthy community included athletics. Sunday, Tuesday, and Thursday were set aside for sports. The community built tennis courts in addition to the wooden stadium for baseball on their vast lands. William Plummer himself played baseball at school while he was growing up. According to communal lore, the team he started was originally called the Belleville Clod Hoppers, then the Belleville Industrial School team, and then the Belleville Grays, named after the attractive, professionally made gray uniforms that Plummer purchased, but possibly also in tribute to Cumberland Posey's Homestead Grays, who were gaining a national reputation for their fine play in the Negro Leagues. The Belleville team prided itself on using only the best equipment. They played every Sunday afternoon throughout the 1920s, and community members who attended as children remember the games being festive occasions that drew two to three thousand people from the local black community who would come to watch and picnic on the grounds. The games played an important role in providing entertainment for the local black community, which in the Jim

Crow South had few opportunities for public social gatherings, especially on Sundays. Owning their own stadium and fielding a high-quality team was an important part of the public contributions the "Saints" (as they were known) made to the black community of Virginia in that era.[6]

The team is first mentioned in the sports pages of the Norfolk *Journal and Guide* (the local African American newspaper) in 1924 as the Belleville Industrial School. When Plummer organized the team, all the players were community members and Plummer's three sons all played. William Plummer was not interested in baseball as a business. Under his leadership the team played for recreation and competition in the local community, as did the other teams of white Hebrews in that era. But in December 1931 William H. Plummer died, and new leadership in Belleville would change the Belleville Grays into a team that would take a surprising role in the history of black baseball.

Howard Z. Plummer succeeded his father as the communal leader. He was thirty-two years old. H. Z. Plummer faced a difficult challenge early in his leadership, as an article in the popular African American magazine *The Crisis* described the Belleville community as "communistic" and a "cult." H. Z. responded in an article he wrote for the *Pittsburgh Courier,* which corrected the "inaccurate and unfair statements about the Church of God and Saints of Christ." He described the Industrial School, chartered by the State of Virginia, which welcomed nonmember students who studied "entirely free from any religious constraint." The experience of being criticized in such a high-profile venue combined with a general lack of understanding of Hebrew Israelite traditions made Plummer's community wary of discussing their beliefs in public and very protective of their privacy. But it also made him seek out ways to bring positive attention to other aspects of communal life. The Belleville Grays would serve this purpose at the end of the decade. The team continued to bring crowds to "the Saints place," but most local people were unaware that the community identified as Israelites.[7]

In 1932 the *Journal and Guide* began to refer to the team as the "Grays of the Belleville Industrial School." One of their star pitchers, Josiah Wagner, was raised at the school. Josiah's son, Joel, remembered his father's stories of traveling with the team and their refusal to play on the Jewish Sabbath. Plummer began to professionalize the team. They trained in Florida and became members of the Tidewater Associated League. The Grays toured that summer, winning many games including one against another Jewish team from the Paterson, New Jersey Young Men's Hebrew Association, as the newspaper recounted: "On Sunday the Grays batt[l]ed the Y.M.H.A of Paterson [NJ] and defeated the Yiddish boys by batting the pill to all corners of the lot."[8]

H. Z. Plummer brought other changes to the Belleville Grays. For the first time in 1932, local baseball players who were not raised in the community joined the team. Pitcher Roy Watford and second baseman Albert "Buster" Haywood came from a renowned local team, the Portsmouth Firefighters. Borrowing players for important games was common in independent baseball, although it was a controversial practice in the Negro Leagues. The top-quality players who were paid per game and not under contract moved around to make additional money and help teams win. Plummer's brother Judah, an excellent catcher, also played for the Firefighters, as did the best-known Negro League player from the Portsmouth area, Buck Leonard. In his autobiography, Leonard credits Buster Haywood with cautioning him not to leave the relatively well-paid and steady opportunities to try out for Ben Taylor's Baltimore Stars where the players were paid a percentage of the gate rather than a salary. But Leonard did leave, and Haywood was himself enticed a few years later to seek more competitive and lucrative opportunities. In 1935 Haywood went to Jacksonville to try out for a new professional team that would become part of the Negro National League, the Brooklyn (later Newark) Eagles, owned by Abe and Effa Manley and managed by the same Ben Taylor (1888–1953). Taylor was one of the Taylor brothers who played a prominent role in early black baseball. Taylor was a stellar first baseman and also managed for many years for a number of Negro League teams. He was elected to the Baseball Hall of Fame in 2006. These contacts would encourage Plummer's interest in league play and would bring his team attention outside the Portsmouth area.[9]

H. Z. PLUMMER AND THE BUSINESS OF BLACK BASEBALL

The instability of league structures made the line between playing independently and in leagues fluid. Teams and individual players shifted between league and independent play, even during the course of a season. New leagues formed and dissolved frequently. From 1938–1940 that fluid pattern was illustrated by the Belleville Grays. The experience of this team is indicative of the difficulties involved in attaining status in the business of black baseball. H. Z. Plummer would gain respect for his own business dealings from the black press, although his aspirations to gain national recognition for the Belleville Grays would be tempered by the realities of the business of black baseball.

Plummer saw building the Belleville Grays as a positive investment that would bring respect to his community, make an economic contribution to the region, and bring honor to the race. E. B. Rea, sports editor of the leading black newspaper in Virginia, the Norfolk *Journal and Guide*, admired Plummer's goals. He praised Plummer and the team and urged fans to support them. He pointed out the financial benefits organized black baseball brought to the community, noting that each team carried twenty-two players, as well as a business and managerial staff that kept black men employed in hard times. He also reminded his readers that this work, "is not of the lowest calling, but a part of the national entertainment offered throughout the country." Baseball carried prestige and status. Plummer believed this effort to build his team would bring recognition and acceptance to his community and refute the idea that his group was "communistic" or a cult.[10]

The team began to travel extensively and received attention as a potential league competitor. Being involved in league play and travel would be difficult to do while at the same time respecting their religious commitments, but Plummer made every effort. Benjamin H. Young, community member and now manager of the team, announced in the black press that they were looking for opponents and they would play "any day excepting Friday and Saturday." He also noted that they hired local star Eugene "Sook" Lawrence and brought the former Negro League catcher Buster Haywood, who had played for them in the early 1930s, back to their squad to underline their commitment to high-quality baseball. When they returned from a trip to play teams in North Carolina, H. Z. Plummer commented, "The club is getting along fine, but it is not quite up to standard. But before I have finished I am going to place a team in the field second to none." The newspaper pointed out that Plummer "travels with the team and appears in uniform at every game. He is a former star of Belleville teams of the good old days." To prepare for league play, Plummer scheduled contests against high-caliber teams such as Ben Taylor's Washington Royal Giants; the Baltimore Black Sox; and two Negro League teams, the New York Black Yankees and Alex Pompez's New York Cubans.[11]

To further the plans, Plummer hired a local booking agent with national connections, John B. (Brady) Johnson, to arrange games. Johnson attempted to schedule contests for the Grays with the Negro League's Pittsburgh Crawfords and the Newark Eagles. In a letter to Abe Manley of the Eagles, Johnson claimed the Grays were the "best club" in the area, perhaps not as strong as the Negro National League clubs, but "a big favorite" in Norfolk and Portsmouth. As part of the offer, Plummer would provide guest accommodations at the Belleville Industrial School and suggested a one-hundred-dollar guarantee with options of a 40 percent net for the visiting team. Although there are no records of the Grays playing either the Eagles or the Crawfords that season, former Crawford catcher Leon Ruffin was added to the lineup late in the season, as H. Z. Plummer began to look for players who could fulfill his promise of making the Grays "second to none."[12]

Leon Ruffin came from Portsmouth and grew up around the port's deep-sea fishing. He came home after the 1938 season, leaving the Pittsburgh Crawfords when the team moved to Toledo. Ruffin was a catcher with a strong arm. He played for the Newark Eagles in 1936, 1939, 1942–43 and, after serving in the Navy, was the starting catcher for the Newark Eagles in 1946 when they won the Negro League championship. Adding Ruffin to the team at the end of the season foreshadowed the efforts Plummer would make in the 1939 season to build the Belleville Grays into a contending team.[13]

In 1939 Plummer continued his plans to make the Belleville Grays a top ballclub. In January, the black press reported that one of the local teams the Grays played against, the Washington Royal Giants, was planning to seek admission to the Negro National League (NNL). The application was brought to the January meeting of NNL owners but tabled until the spring. Instead of waiting for a decision from the NNL, Royal Giants owner W. M. Josephs decided to join a new league instead, consisting of teams from Virginia, North Carolina, and the Washington, DC area, to be known as the Negro International League. John Brady Johnson, the man who promoted games for the Belleville Grays in 1938, was named president. H. Z. Plummer agreed to serve as treasurer and enter the Belleville Grays into this league. They announced their intention to play a split season, from May 1 to July 4 and then July 4 to Labor Day, with a championship series between the winners of the two halves, as was customary in the Negro National and American Leagues. Seven teams joined, including the Washington Royal Giants, managed by the former Negro League star and future Hall of Fame member Ben Taylor. His involvement was an indication of the seriousness and high level of expectations for the league effort. Plummer and his associates were hoping to create the "third colored diamond body," to rival the Negro National and American Leagues.[14]

In keeping with their new status, the Belleville Grays would also be managed by a former Negro League player, "Sleepy" Joe Lewis. Lewis, who came from Maryland, was a catcher for the Lincoln Giants, Baltimore Black Sox, the Bacharachs and the Hilldales in the 1920s. He caught the attention of sportswriter Rollo Wilson, who called him a "hard-working and conscientious athlete" who was often the backup catcher for stars like Biz Mackey. He settled in Portsmouth and became manager of the Belleville Grays, serving in that position in 1939 and 1940.

Plans to organize the league continued. Brady Johnson again sought games for the Grays with Negro National League teams the Homestead Grays, Newark Eagles, New York Cubans, and New York Black Yankees. In March the Grays went to Jacksonville, Florida for spring training. Final plans for the league were made at a meeting at the end of April. At the meeting Plummer, along with the owner of the Baltimore Black Sox, Joseph Thomas, suggested the league's name be changed to the Eastern Colored League. Plummer's and Thomas's argument was that calling the league "international" created a false impression for "an organization operated among players of one race and in one section of the country." Plummer and Thomas prevailed, and the name was changed. To those aware of Negro League history, the new name would echo the Eastern Colored League that was organized in the 1920s by Ed Bolden to compete with Rube Foster's Negro National League, and perhaps that was what they had in mind. The organization also developed plans to play

Tidewater area games at stadiums in Portsmouth used primarily by local white minor league teams, Bain Field and Sewanee Field, not at the old Belleville grandstands. They also agreed that each team would carry sixteen players. Umpires would be paid and selected by the home team, and the gate would be divided sixty-forty between the home and away team.[15]

The Grays played exceptionally well in the month of May in league games, posting a record of nine wins and two defeats. A team photo in the *Journal and Guide* ran under the caption "Leaders in the Eastern Colored League." In a short time Plummer had achieved the prominence and national attention for the team he had hoped for. D. E. Ellis, columnist for the *New York Age* reported small crowds for these games, despite their high caliber of play, and exhorted his readers to support "Negro teams of the Eastern Colored League, and their associates, instead of crowding into the ofay [white] parks." Competition from white baseball would continue to plague all the black leagues despite the high quality of the black game.[16]

To build a strong team, Plummer invited players who were not part of the Belleville community to supplement his own community members. In addition to Roy Watford and Buster Haywood, who had played for the team in prior years, Plummer added pitchers Vernon "Big Six" Riddick, Tony Spruill, Lefty Stewart, and Gentry Jessup. Position players James "Rip" Wilson, James Mickey, and Tommy Sampson were also recruited. But community members were actively involved. William Plummer and Jesse Jose would serve as umpires for the league. Luke Fears, Jasper Elam, and Calvin Wooten (a relative of COGASOC founder William Saunders Crowdy) played regularly. The star pitcher was Belleville community member Nathaniel "Sonny" Jeffries, who went on to play in the Negro Leagues before and after a stint in the Army in World War II, and was given a tryout for the white International League St. Louis Cardinals' farm team in 1950 after baseball's integration. Most other community members were reluctant to try out at higher levels, however, as leaving would undermine their connections to their religious community and challenge their religious observances.[17]

This team stayed together for the rest of the season, but not as part of the Eastern Colored League. Although high level Negro League play was most desirable, high-level Negro League business made Plummer uneasy. The controversy that caused Plummer to withdraw his team from the league began in late May when Ben Taylor's Royal Giants beat the Grays 6–3, with Sonny Jeffries taking the loss at Griffith Stadium, Washington's major league ballpark. The Royal Giants also played and won a second game against the High Point Red Sox from a rival league that day.

Finding it peculiar that the Royal Giants would play the High Point Sox and the Grays the same day, sports columnist Sam Lacy investigated the matter. He learned that the Belleville management (and particularly Plummer as a league officer) was disturbed at a report from the team in Charlotte that the management of the Royal Giants had padded expenses for advertising and the cost of balls when they played in North Carolina. The Grays announced that they would not play the Royal Giants unless the dispute about expenditures could be resolved, so the Giant owners secured a second game against the Red Sox in case the Grays did not come to Washington.

The Royal Giants' backup plan to substitute the High Point team disturbed Plummer even more because it undermined the integrity of league play. On Friday morning before the game, Bishop Plummer and Benjamin Young traveled to Griffith Stadium for a discussion with representatives of the Royal Giants (Josephs and Taylor) hoping to resolve the dispute. Washington Senator owner Clark Griffith negotiated a settlement between the clubs, and Plummer agreed to have his team return to Washington on Sunday to play. Plummer closed the session, according to Lacy. "'I do not want to let it be said that my club disappointed the Washington fans or failed to live up to its pledge to the league,' the bishop said." But having to negotiate petty controversy deeply disturbed Plummer's sense of propriety and his religious principles concerning fair play. That would be the last league game the Belleville Grays played.[18]

Although Plummer's experience with league play was difficult, it enhanced his national reputation as an honest businessman and gentleman. The same edition of the weekly Baltimore *Afro-American* that carried Lacy's report made the official announcement that three teams pulled out of the Eastern Colored League: the Belleville Grays, Norfolk Black Tars, and the Baltimore Black Sox. The next week, the *Afro-American* reported other inappropriate financial dealings, this time involving league president John Brady Johnson, and secretary W. M. Josephs. During the winter when the league was getting organized, Josephs paid Johnson's hotel bill in exchange for using his influence to get the Giants into the league in place of a local rival. Josephs also took seventy-five dollars from the owner of the Giants, James Page, for the franchise fee, but that fee was never paid to the league. The *New York Age* also covered the story and lauded Plummer's decision to leave. "Bishop Plummer, founder and generally acknowledged backbone of the league . . . [is] to be commended for not tolerating 'unclean' dealings."[19]

The Belleville Grays finished their schedule as an independent team. They ended the season with a 45–8 record, playing other local independent and some Negro League teams. They did finally meet the Newark Eagles and lost to them by a score of 3–1 in early July. Darrell Howard, in his study of black baseball in Virginia, commented: "It was a rarity for the professionals to play the locals during a promoted tour, but Belleville's reputation now preceded it." In his estimation the loss "highlighted the prowess of Belleville as they were able to hold a professional team to a respectable margin."[20] The Grays were scheduled to play the Eagles again in August, according to a telegram from Abe Manley to Brady Johnson who, despite his continuing affiliation with the league, still handled booking arrangements for Plummer's team. The games were to take place in Norfolk on August eighth through the tenth. Belleville was to provide a hundred-dollar guarantee, with an option of 40 percent net for the visiting team, with lodging at Belleville. There are no records to verify that the second series of games took place, however.

Plummer's experience with Negro League play left him alienated from black baseball's power elite and their business practices. While other owners either overlooked or were themselves involved in the petty financial disagreements that were common in a small business like the Negro Leagues, Plummer wanted no part of it. As a religious leader he was not comfortable with the kind of shady dealings that were required and would not allow himself or his team to be part of that world.[21]

Bishop Plummer made one more attempt at league play in 1940, in response to an invitation from *Afro-American* sports editor, Art Carter, who was organizing a new Interstate League. Plummer's indecisive behavior around this invitation was a clear indication of his ambivalence about making another effort at league play. Carter sent a letter to Plummer in March about the plans for the best teams in Maryland and Virginia to form a minor league for the Negro National and American Leagues. Carter also invited Dr. Joseph Thomas, now head of the Edgewater Black Sox in Baltimore and Plummer's close associate, to join; Thomas agreed immediately while Plummer failed to reply for some time.[22]

Manager Joe Lewis finally communicated with Carter on behalf of Bishop Plummer, indicating that the Grays would join the league in time for the season's start on May 26. They played their first game, but Plummer, hesitating still, had not paid the franchise fee. Carter sent several letters to Lewis asking for the financial commitment, but it was not forthcoming until Carter wrote to Plummer directly. Carter's letter indicated that he had spoken both to Lewis and to Plummer's friend John Murphy, owner of the *Afro-American* and Carter's boss, about Plummer's doubts. Carter acknowledged that both he and Dr. Thomas knew that Plummer might be hesitant after the difficult situation last year. But he reassured him that no one who was involved in the league the prior year, except Dr. Thomas, would be connected with the new league. The letter, dated Friday, June 8, received an immediate response. Plummer came up to Washington on Sunday, paid the franchise fee, and fixed a schedule of play.[23]

The Grays played well enough but were not the team they had been the prior year. With the exception of community member and outfielder Mark Hill, the team was composed primarily of young college men from the Portsmouth region. At the end of July they had won four and lost four in league play and were in third place. Earlier in July, Joe Lewis thought they would have to drop out of league play because they couldn't always find enough personnel for the Sunday games. Although as victors of a late season tournament they were named the official state champions of Virginia, the 1940 season was not a successful one for the Grays. The Interstate League folded at the end of August. [24]

Yet H. Z. Plummer's influence gained him a strong reputation as an honest man who would be an asset to the Negro Leagues if he wished to become more involved. Plummer's commitment to the game was brought to national attention that summer by *Pittsburgh Courier* reporter Randy Dixon, who thought Plummer could resolve the fights among owners that plagued the Negro National League:

> There's an esteemed gentleman with dough and a patriot's love of the game, who is willing and eager to enter a league with them. He's Bishop Plummer of ecclesiastical fame. . . . The entry of . . . Plummer into the pastime would prove bromatic. [The] Manleys . . . have transformed Newark into the sepia baseball capital of the nation. . . . With Plummer . . . in tow, if such be the case, and with Cum Posey always playing ball with the top man, perhaps a new and needed order of things will evolve.[25]

This high praise did not persuade Plummer. Although he achieved his goal of creating a team that was for a brief time "second to none" in Virginia, he would take the effort no further. Plummer's business adventure with organized black baseball had come to an end. H. Z. Plummer was not inclined to become the arbiter of the very difficult relationships between the owners of the Negro League teams.

The story of the Belleville Grays illuminates the experiences of a religious group negotiating the world of sport in the segregated South. Plummer saw building the Belleville Grays as a positive investment that would bring respect to his community, make an economic contribution to the Tidewater region, and bring credit to the race. H. Z. Plummer's efforts gained attention in the sports pages of the black press, both locally and nationally, although his aspirations to gain national recognition for the Belleville Grays would be tempered by the realities of the business of black baseball, which conflicted with his values. The team achieved a short-lived success in black baseball but was soon alienated from an industry's cut-throat business dealings that were an anathema to the religious values of Temple Beth El.

ACTIVITIES

ACTIVITY 1

Reenact the meeting between the Royal Giants and Belleville Grays leadership. What arguments did they present? What religious values might

Plummer have used in his position? Do you think religious values mattered to the Royal Giants owners? How might they have reacted to Plummer?

ACTIVITY 2

What do you imagine the correspondence between Art Carter (the journalist who was starting a new league) and Bishop Plummer to consist of? Write your own version of Carter's letter and Plummer's reply. What arguments might Carter have used to persuade Plummer to give it one more try?

ACTIVITY 3

Should sports make room for religious values? Research another case where religion and sports have come into conflict over Sabbath or holy day observance and compare it to this one. You might use the example of Christian Olympic runner Eric Liddell in the film *Chariots of Fire* or Jewish baseball pitcher Sandy Koufax's decision not to pitch in the World Series on Yom Kippur.

RESOURCES

Alpert, Rebecca. *Out of Left Field: Jews and Black Baseball.* New York: Oxford University Press, 2011.

Church of God and Saints of Christ, and Historical Committee. *History of the Church of God and Saints of Christ.* Suffolk, VA: The Church, 1992.

Dvorak, Katherine. "After Apocalypse, Moses." In John B. Boles, *Masters and Slaves in the House of the Lord: Race and Religion in the American South, 1740–1870,* 173–191. Lexington: University Press of Kentucky, 1988.

Heaphy, Leslie A. *The Negro Leagues, 1869–1960.* Jefferson, NC: McFarland, 2003.

Howard, Darrell J. *"Sunday Coming": Black Baseball in Virginia.* Jefferson, NC: McFarland, 2002.

Inter-university Consortium for Political and Social Research, ed. *Censuses of Religious Bodies, 1906–1936 United States Department of Commerce Bureau of the Census.* Ann Arbor, MI: Inter-university Consortium for Political and Social Research, 1984.

Levine, Lawrence W. *Black Culture and Black Consciousness: Afro-American Folk Thought from Slavery to Freedom.* New York: Oxford University Press, 1977.

Leonard, Buck, and James A. Riley. *Buck Leonard: The Black Lou Gehrig: The Hall of Famer's Story in His Own Words.* New York: Carroll & Graf, 1995.

Martin, Alfred M., and Alfred T. Martin. *The Negro Leagues in New Jersey: A History.* Jefferson, NC: McFarland, 2008.

Raboteau, Albert J. *Slave Religion: The "Invisible Institution" in the Antebellum South.* New York: Oxford University Press, 1980.

CASE 9

Mahmoud Abdul-Rauf
and the National Anthem Ritual
in the NBA

Fig. 9.1. Denver Nuggets guard Mahmoud Abdul-Rauf stands with his teammates and prays during the national anthem. AP Photo/Michael S. Green.

GOAL: To examine the compromise between religious belief and public image for high profile athletes.

During the 1995–1996 season Mahmoud Abdul-Rauf was the leading scorer for the Denver Nuggets of the National Basketball Association (NBA). In March of that season fans began to notice that Abdul-Rauf was either not present or not standing at attention during the pregame ritual of the singing of the "Star-Spangled Banner." The topic surfaced on a local sports radio program, a firestorm of media attention ensued, and the NBA took action. They informed Abdul-Rauf that according to the players' union contract he was obligated to follow league rules, including the following: "Players, coaches and trainers are to stand and line up in a dignified posture along the sidelines or the foul line during the playing of the national anthem." Abdul-Rauf refused and was suspended indefinitely without pay. After missing one game (and losing $31,707), Abdul-Rauf agreed to a compromise. He would stand with his teammates, but pray silently for "those who are suffering," holding his hands in front of his face (a gesture Muslims assume in prayer). The Players' Union, in a show of support, reimbursed the fine, and the season resumed. But Abdul-Rauf's life and career would never be the same.

Mahmoud Abdul-Rauf (whose birth name was Chris Jackson) was raised in poverty by his African American mother in Gulfport, Mississippi. He also lived with Tourette's syndrome, a genetic disease that causes involuntary twitching and vocalizations. A basketball scholarship took him to Louisiana State University (LSU). In an in-depth interview in 2007, Abdul-Rauf discussed the experiences in college that radicalized him, including having to pay for tickets for his mother to come see him play and having the Athletics Office call to scold him for wearing the wrong brand of shoes in a photo essay about him in *Sports Illustrated*.[1] But LSU was also where he learned about the history of African American oppression and where his coach introduced him to *The Autobiography of Malcolm X*, the book that would change his life.

He was a star at LSU and taken third in the first round of the 1990 draft by the Denver Nuggets. But he had trouble acclimating to life in the NBA. He gained weight and played poorly. At the same time, he continued to be inspired by Malcolm and tentatively began the process of becoming a Muslim. He met with Muslim leaders, became involved in a *masjid* (mosque), took Arabic lessons, began to pray five times daily, and observed the fast of Ramadan. He completed the process in 1993 when he changed his name and undertook hajj, the pilgrimage to Mecca. He also requested that his wife Kim begin to veil and comport herself modestly, but his wife was not interested in taking on Muslim practices and their marriage ended in divorce. His growing connection to Islam took place in the shadow of the first World Trade Center bombing. America was becoming more aware of Islam, but also more wary, beginning to associate Muslims with terrorists.

The following season his play improved markedly, and he credited his connection to Allah and the structured life he found through Islam. Along with the improved play, some of his practices made for ruptures in his life as a basketball player. His new name kept him from obtaining endorsements. He refused to shower with his teammates, citing Muslim rules about modesty. When his Ramadan fast coincided with mid-season, his teammates worried that fasting would affect his ability to play. He requested a separate prayer space in the locker room. And he stood apart socially, following the rules of his faith, which prohibited smoking, drinking, and gambling. He preferred the company of people he was meeting through the *masjid.*

In the winter of 1995 Abdul-Rauf told the Nuggets that he could no longer participate in the national anthem pregame ritual. He understood it to be a sacred ceremony; he saw the flag as a symbol of a nationalistic faith that was contrary to Islam. He interpreted the patriotic ceremony as getting in the way of his direct connection to Allah. The NBA encouraged him to absent himself. Following his beliefs, he mostly remained in the locker room until the ceremony ended. On some occasions he was present for the ceremony, but ignored it, performing warm-up stretches. The following March his behavior drew the attention of fans who interpreted it as a political act of defiance and not an act of religious conscience.

When questioned about this by the media, Abdul-Rauf further explained that the flag was, to him, a "symbol of oppression, of tyranny."

When the media and fan response erupted, Abdul-Rauf, issued the following statement:

> In the name of God most gracious, most merciful.
>
> In light of my decision not to participate in the national anthem, I have prepared a brief statement to clarify my position.
>
> My intentions were not in any way to be disrespectful to those who regard the national anthem as a sacred ceremony. I am an African-American, a citizen of this country, and one who respects freedom of speech and freedom of expression.
>
> I am also a man who tries to perfect my life on and off the court, and someone who tries to be sincere in my treatment of my fellow human beings, and sincere in any activity that I undertake. Therefore, it is my understanding that 100 percent honesty and sincerity is the requirement for participation in the national anthem. As such, I chose not to disrespect anyone and remain in the locker room or hallway area while the anthem was being played.
>
> I have been undertaking this action for the past 60 games. I made a conscious decision not to make this a public issue. This became a public issue only when the press approached me and made it a public issue. From this point on, it is my intention to try and live a peaceful life, play basketball, and perfect my humanity to the highest level possible.
>
> Peace be upon you, and may God bless you all.[2]

In times before the Internet and social media allowed for everyone to express an opinion, television, radio, newspapers, and magazines were the primary public outlets for discussing Abdul-Rauf's action, and, because the story made headlines, Abdul-Rauf received many letters, including death threats and suggestions that he "go back to Africa." While many fans expressed hostility, especially on Denver radio talk shows, others shared more positive views. Some pointed to the irony of proclaiming that, in a country that honored free expression of beliefs, Abdul-Rauf was being punished for his. As John D. Knopf from New York wrote in a succinct March 24, 1996 letter to the sports editor of the *New York Times*, "The reason why I stand up during the playing of the national anthem is that we have the right to sit down." Muslims were called on to explain why standing for the national anthem would violate their religious beliefs. The leading Muslim player in the NBA, Hakeem Olajuwon of the Houston Rockets, declared that to him the most important Muslim value was respect for and obedience to the laws of the nation in which one lives and that he did not understand Abdul-Rauf's position.[3] Scholar Aminah Beverly McCloud pointed out that, like other religions, Islam is diverse and its precepts are open to a variety of interpretations.[4] This perspective was borne out when the Council on American-Islamic Relations noted that standing for the anthem was not outlawed in Islam,[5] but the Society for Adherence to the Sunna issued a legal ruling supporting Abdul-Rauf's position.[6]

There was much discussion about Abdul-Rauf's rights. According to one legal opinion, his actions would have been supported under Title VII of the Civil Rights Act of 1964, which protects an employee from discrimination based on religious belief or practice as long as it doesn't pose a hardship on the employer. The author did leave open the possibility that if fans stopped coming and sponsors withdrew it would pose an undue burden on the Nuggets, however.[7]

The compromise was enacted and media attention quieted down, except for one incident. Four staff members of the sports radio station KPBI in Denver went to the Colorado Islamic Center, the *masjid* where Abdul-Rauf prayed and played the national anthem on a bugle and trumpet. The incident sparked outrage, the station apologized, and the offenders were punished. But Abdul-Rauf was no longer welcome in Denver. He was traded to the Sacramento Kings the following season, where he spent two years, then went on to play in Turkey, for a year with the Vancouver Grizzlies, and then spent the rest of his career playing in Russia, Italy, Greece, Saudi Arabia, and finally Japan. He returned to Gulfport, remarried, and raised a family. He turned a former crack house into a mosque where he served as imam for forty families. The mosque was vandalized repeatedly, burned down by the Ku Klux Klan, and ultimately destroyed by Hurricane Katrina. Abdul-Rauf's family moved to Atlanta in 2005.

Abdul-Rauf would no longer be known for his incredible basketball skills as an offensive guard and league-leading free throw shooter, overcoming the difficulties of growing up in poverty, learning how to live with a debilitating disease, or living a holy life in a world full of temptations to sexual and financial excess. Instead, Mahmoud Abdul-Rauf's name became synonymous with this case and the complexities of patriotism and religion in sport.

ACTIVITIES

ACTIVITY 1

- Watch the film *By the Dawns Early Light: Chris Jackson's Journey to Islam*, directed by Zareena Grewal. Summarize the views of fans and other players who are interviewed. Which do you find the most compelling and why?
- What are the most important reasons Abdul-Rauf gives for his actions? Do any of them persuade you?
- How does he describe his turn to Islam? What about Malcolm X moved Chris Jackson? How does that conform to values of Islam? What Muslim rituals do you see him participating in? How does he describe the connection between Islam and basketball? What part left the most lasting impression and why?
- Do you see his decision as political or religious? What's the difference?
- Abdul-Rauf calls Muslims who disagree with him "apologetic." What do you think of that argument? What are the arguments that Muslim scholars give that you would quarrel with and why?
- What is the most interesting thing you learned about Islam from this film?
- Do you think "the NBA won"?
- What do you think of Abdul-Rauf's rationale for his compromise?
- How do you relate Abdul-Rauf's experiences to 9/11? What would have been different if he played today?

ACTIVITY 2

Listen to Abdul-Rauf's 2013 talk at the Al Tawheed Center, posted on YouTube.[8] Make a list of questions you would like to ask him in response to his experience and his current perspective.

ACTIVITY 3

Write a blog in response to one of the following questions. You must research the topic first, consulting at least three reliable sources that you will document. Post the blog on the course Web site. Read the blogs posted by other students and respond to three of them. Continue to check the comments, adding at least two more comments to one of the blogs. Check the comments on your blog and respond to as many of them as possible.

- Is singing the national anthem a "sacred ceremony" as Abdul-Rauf claimed?
- Does the Civil Rights Act protect his action?
- Is his action in keeping with Islam?
- Is basketball an appropriate arena to express radical ideas?

ACTIVITY 4

Abdul-Rauf's act has been compared to

- Jehovah's Witnesses' refusal to salute the flag
- Sandy Koufax's refusal to pitch on Yom Kippur
- Muhammad Ali's refusal to be drafted
- Tommie Smith and John Carlos' black power salute at the 1968 Olympics

Find out more about each of those topics. Pick one to compare to Abdul-Rauf's action and explain what makes them either similar or different.

CASE 10

Judo and Hijab at the Olympics

Fig. 10.1. London, Britain—Wojdan Shahrkani of Saudi Arabia competes against Puerto Rico's Melissa Mojica during the first round match in the women's judo over 78-kilogram class at the 2012 London Olympics. Kyodo via AP Images.

GOAL: To examine the connections between Islamic values of modesty and gender segregation as they apply to women's Olympic sports.

Leading up to the 2012 Olympics, the International Olympic Committee (IOC) worked diligently to ensure that the last three countries with all-male teams (Brunei, Qatar, and Saudi Arabia) would include women for the first time. Women's representation in the Olympics was slow to develop overall. No women were allowed to compete in the first modern Olympics in 1896; only eleven were present in Paris in 1900 and only permitted to compete in golf and lawn tennis. In 1912 women competed in swimming for the first time but American women were not allowed as the Amateur Athletic Union would not permit them to participate in events without "proper attire" (long skirts). The situation improved slowly; in 1984 only 25 percent of Olympic participants were women. Judo, the sport we are considering in this case, became an Olympic sport for men in 1964, and not until 1992 for women. Women's overall participation increased to 44 percent by 2012, and women-only sports like netball, softball, and synchronized swimming have also been added, although softball is no longer included. The first year that every country was represented by a woman was 2012, and the IOC was committed to the goal.

Saudi Arabia, which does not have a culture conducive to women's sports activities, was the last country to comply. With the rare exception of a few expensive private organizations, women in Saudi Arabia are not allowed to join sports clubs, most of which are government operated. Schools don't offer physical education classes for girls, and women aren't allowed to attend sporting events in public. Saudi policies were denounced by Human Rights Watch in a report published in 2012, *Steps of the Devil: Denial of Women and Girls' Rights to Sport in Saudi Arabia.* So finding Olympic-level women athletes in this culture is not a simple task. Although one Saudi woman, an equestrian, would have been eligible for competition, her horse was injured. The IOC permitted two Saudi women who did not qualify to compete, as is the Olympic policy when a country has no eligible players to send. One was a runner, Sarah Attar, who was raised in the United States but has dual citizenship. The other was a sixteen-year-old judoko in the 78+kg weight class, Wojdan Ali Seraj Abdulrahim Shahrkhani, from the city of Mecca, who learned her craft from her father, an international judo judge. Although black belt is the standard for Olympic qualifiers, Wojdan had only earned a blue belt (two classes below) at the time.

The Saudi case is not the norm in Muslim countries, whose policies regarding women's sports vary widely. Islam, like all other religions, is not monolithic. Different countries that are predominantly Muslim have different relationships to Islamic law (sharia). And many people who practice Islam live in countries that are not predominantly Muslim and have different ways of incorporating their traditions into their lives. Individual Muslim women athletes have been competing in the Olympics for many years, beginning with Turkish women fencers in 1936. Turkish Muslim women have medaled in judo, including a gold medal in 2012. And women from many conservative Muslim countries (including Libya, Iraq, and Afghanistan) compete in (and win) events wearing hijab. Traditional Islam encourages women to be physically fit, but many Muslim women prefer to achieve that goal in private, in keeping with the goal of modesty. Yet, as Jawad points out, modesty can be interpreted in many ways, and manifested as either internal or external.[1] Muslim women athletes should not be assumed to be flaunting Muslim law or tradition as Olympic competitors, despite criticism they have received from some conservative Muslim clerics.

Modest dress (hijab) is an important criterion for Muslim women (and observant men) participating in sports and in the public sphere. I am using *hijab* as a general term, although covering practices vary; hijab indicates some type of covering of Muslim women's arms, legs, and heads. (Men are required to cover from waist to knee.) Many, but not all, women who practice Islam do wear hijab, for a variety of reasons. Some are required (as in countries like Saudi Arabia), while some are defiant (as in countries like France and Turkey that forbid public covering). Some do it for religious reasons of modesty, and others for a symbolic demonstration of their Muslim identity as a source of pride. Still others wear hijab on some occasions (during Ramadan, other religious observances, or when required) but generally are comfortable appearing uncovered in public. Many Muslim women who want to participate (at least in certain sports) have found ways to accommodate their dress requirements, and some companies are designing hijab with snug-fitting closures to meet the requirements of various sports where loose-fitting garments do not comport with the rules of the game and could cause safety concerns. Recently FIFA has lifted its ban against headscarves in soccer, given the availability of these new styles.[2]

A preference for gender segregation has also complicated Muslim women's participation in international competitions like the Olympics. The fact that sports are also gender segregated allows many Muslims to consider sports a place where they are comfortable in their religious practices. But some conservative interpretations of Islam take gender segregation to mean that women can't play sports in situations where men can observe them (as coaches, officials, or spectators), even if they are covered. This has led to the creation of the International Women's Islamic Games where men are completely excluded from the roles of coaching and officiating as well as spectating. These events actually create opportunities for women coaches and officials. But because schools and other facilities in the Islamic diaspora do not make accommodations for women to play sports in gender-segregated settings, the need for gender segregation has posed hardships for traditional Muslim women to get involved in sport in some societies.

JUDO AND HIJAB AT THE OLYMPICS

Both issues, modest dress and gender segregation, came into play for Wojdan Shahrkhani as she prepared herself to become the first woman representing Saudi Arabia at the 2012 London Olympics. (Track and field competition took place after the judo events, making her the first.) Conservative critics criticized her (and her family) for being willing to participate at all. Her support staff was not a problem, since her father was her coach and her brother served as a bodyguard, and no laws about gender segregation prohibit male family members from accompanying her. But any venue where men would see her perform or act as judges or referees would be considered a violation by those in Saudi Arabia responsible for the strict rules against women's participation in sports.

Shahrkani planned to compete in hijab (traditional judo uniform and additional headscarf to cover her neck and hair). The International Judo Federation's (IJF) president, Marius Vizer, declared that wearing hijab would not be in keeping with the principles and standards of judo. He deemed it dangerous, potentially leading to choking or other safety issues. Throwing opponents by holding onto their clothing (known as grapping) or hair is a fundamental part of judo, and the IJF official saw wearing hijab as potentially creating unfair conditions. All clothing is highly regulated in judo, down to the fiber used for the outfits, as evidenced by the twenty-two-page description in the sports and organization rules of the IJF.[3] But many women have worn hijab to compete in martial arts, including judo, and Shahrkani refused to compete without hijab. Because this was such a high-profile case, the IOC stepped in and negotiated a compromise between the IJF and the Saudi Olympics Committee (SOC). Instead of traditional hijab, Shahrkani was permitted to wear a tight cap and pull her uniform high on her neck.

The bout took place on August 3, 2012, and was over in eighty-two seconds, longer than the shortest match in the elimination round, which was forty-eight seconds. She was defeated by ippon, or the judo equivalent of a knockout, by the thirteenth-ranked judoko in her class, Melissa Mojica (a twenty-eight year old from Puerto Rico). As described by the New York Times, Mojica "cleanly executed a technique called a side-drop, in which she dropped to the floor and pulled Shahrkani down over her leg."[4] Mojica later commented that the cap Shahrkani wore was irrelevant, as was the issue of her religion. In her response after the match, Shahrkani said she was nervous, both because of the highly publicized circumstances and the hijab debate, but that she was happy to have represented Saudi women and was looking forward to the opportunities her example could create for others in the future. The event was not broadcast on Saudi television, and because it coincided with Friday afternoon prayers many Muslims did not see it even on satellite broadcast where it was available.

But there was strong reaction around the world and in Saudi Arabia, with some hailing it as a great accomplishment for Saudi women while others calling it an abomination and disgrace.

ACTIVITIES

ACTIVITY 1

Divide into groups of four to recreate the decision-making process that will decide whether to allow Shahrkhani to enter the match in hijab. In each group, randomly select a representative of the IJF, IOC, and the SOC, with one person serving as moderator. Then gather as groups for each role to formulate your arguments (and, for the moderators, your tactics for organizing the conversation). Return to your first groups and decide. In the large group discuss the final outcome. Did you come to the same compromise that permitted Shahrkhani to play in an improvised head covering? What other solutions might have resulted?

ACTIVITY 2A

Write responses to the following five comments. Your responses should present opposing arguments and you should include at least three reasons in each response.

- Saudi traditionalist tweet: "Whores of the Olympics. . . . They want to run so that they intentionally fall down and reveal (their figures)."
- Human Rights Watch representative: "an eleventh hour change of course to avoid a ban does not alter the dismal and unequal conditions for women and girls in Saudi Arabia."[5]
- "It is beautiful that she played and in front of people and proved her presence and stated that Saudi women are not all servants at home," said Wajeha al-Huwaidir, a Saudi activist who launched a campaign before the 2008 Beijing Olympics to support women's participation.

- Saudi preacher Sittam al-Dusri told the Associated Press that Shahrkhani's family should have protected her "as a precious gem" from the eyes of men.
- "I don't think that will lead to concrete changes led by the Saudi government," he (Christoph Wilcke, a Saudi researcher) said. Wilcke saw the event as encouragement to Saudi women to continue their efforts to "take matters into their own hands."[6]

ACTIVITY 2B

After responding to these perspectives, explain which one is closest to your own. What are your reasons for subscribing to this perspective? If you were going to tweet your own view after this event, what would you write?

ACTIVITY 3

Make a list of the stereotypes of Muslim women that come up in the course of this case. Did this case help or hurt representations of Muslim women? Why? Did the case change your perceptions in any way?

ACTIVITY 4

Write a letter to Shahrkhani with advice for the future in her religious life and her sporting life. Does the question of dress detract from the question of sports abilities? Which would you advise her to focus on? How should she deal with her detractors? Do you think she should become an activist for women's rights?

RESOURCES

Benn, Tansin, Gertrud Pfister, and Haifaa Jawad, eds. *Muslim Women and Sport.* New York: Routledge, 2011.
Muslim Women in Sport Foundation. http://www.mwsf.org.uk/.

PART 4

RELIGION AND ETHICAL DILEMMAS IN SPORTS

Sports have been dealing with ethical issues related to violence, performance enhancement, and equal opportunity in recent years. The cases in this final part of *Religion and Sports* will ask whether the ethical perspectives provided by religious traditions have anything to contribute to the public conversation on these issues. Case 11 looks at the decision of the Catholic Church hierarchy in Pennsylvania to allow an eleven-year-old girl, Caroline Pla, to play football on a boys' Catholic Youth Organization team after first denying her request to do so. The case provides an opportunity to ask not only if girls should be playing in the same leagues as boys but also examines the current controversy over whether children should be allowed to play contact football at all. In case 12 we will look at requests that the Catholic Church condemn bullfighting in Spain to think through possible opportunities for religions to pursue strategies that mitigate unnecessary violence in our world. Case 13 concerns the Florida State University Seminoles football team, who have gained legal rights to the name, logo, and mascot that belong to the Seminole tribe of

Florida and Oklahoma to examine the relationship between the U.S. government and native tribes as mediated through sports. Case 14 is about a "basketball blowout" and asks whether it was good sportsmanship for the Grinnell men's basketball team to "run up the score" in their game against Faith Baptist Bible College so that their star player, Jack Taylor, himself an evangelical Christian, could score a record 138 points. We conclude with a case that features the renowned basketball player and coach and executive Phil Jackson, also known for his spiritual contributions to sports, and ask, "what would Phil Jackson do?" when confronted with the dilemmas we've examined in the case studies.

CASE 11

Caroline Pla and CYO Football

SHOULD GIRLS BE ALLOWED TO COMPETE WITH BOYS?

Fig. 11.1. Caroline Pla and her teammates. Courtesy of Seal Pla.

GOAL: To assess the campaign waged by an eleven-year-old girl for the right to play football with boys in a Catholic league.

In the other cases we have looked at involving women's sports, the fact that most sports are gender segregated was not only assumed but viewed as an asset for religious reasons. The fact that Philadelphia had sex-segregated education in its parochial school system created the opportunity for women's basketball to flourish in the 1940s. Even the most traditional Muslims permit women's sports as long as men are not involved, and that eased the way for bringing women from traditional Muslim countries into the Olympics as we saw in case 10. But in this circumstance religious objections to sex-integrated sports are a point of contention that galvanized many forces and drew much public scrutiny.

In 2012 Caroline Pla was an eleven-year-old girl living in Doylestown, Pennsylvania. Pla comes from a family of practicing Catholics and passionate football fans. Caroline played with her brothers until the age of five, when she became involved in a Pop Warner coed youth football team. Although only a small number of girls play on majority boys' teams, studies suggests that there is no reason to segregate children playing sports by gender before puberty. The point was proven in dramatic fashion when a thirteen-year-old African American girl, Mo'ne Davis, pitched a shutout in the 2014 Little League World Series and became the youngest person ever to appear on the cover of *Sports Illustrated*. The bodies of young boys and girls are of comparable weights and strength. Most of the time, Pla's family pointed out, no one knew she was a girl until she removed her helmet.

In fifth grade, Pla joined her friends as they moved to her church's Catholic Youth Organization (CYO) team, the Our Lady of Mt. Carmel Romans. The CYO, established in 1930 by Bishop Bernard Sheil in Chicago, was designed to create opportunities for Catholic youth to play competitive sports. In its early years it provided venues in predominantly Catholic neighborhoods for organized activities to help immigrant youth assimilate to American culture in protected environments. Basketball and boxing were most popular, but as the CYO grew they developed programs in a wide variety of sports. While the original goal is no longer maintained, CYO has continued to provide reasonably priced, high-quality youth sports programs that reflect Catholic values. Although some dioceses, including western Pennsylvania, permit CYO football programs to be coed, and other dioceses switched to coed flag football to avoid the contact issues, the Philadelphia chapter plays contact football and has a rule against allowing girls to play with boys in contact sports. But no one mentioned this rule at the time Pla signed up in 2011. It is surprising the rule was not invoked, because in 2004 Ashley Brown, a sixth grader from Upper Darby, was also informed by the same diocese that she was not allowed to play based on the rule in the handbook, which officials interpreted as a safety measure. Brown hired a lawyer. Despite a fair amount of public support in the media including a strong statement from a professional woman's football team, the Delaware Griffins, the diocese stood firm, and Brown turned to other sports. (She later attended Immaculata College for a nursing degree.)[1]

But when Caroline signed up she was permitted to play. She became a star and respected team member; a varsity player and all-star at defensive end and guard on offense. In the middle of her second year, Caroline's coach was informed that the Philadelphia area CYO handbook prohibited girls because football was "a full contact sport designed for boys." Citing safety concerns, the diocesan official responsible for CYO, Jason Budd, told her coach and parents she had to quit immediately, but they persuaded him to allow her to complete the season. We do not know who reported the handbook infraction, but media reports speculated that it was some parent from an opposing team. Budd initially told them the ruling was final, but the archbishop of Philadelphia, Charles Chaput, decided to review the policy. He convened a panel of experts that included coaches, parents, religious leaders, and doctors to make a recommendation to him.

With the support of her teammates, parents, coach, and parish priest, Caroline began a campaign to get her voice heard in the process. She began with phone calls and e-mails to Budd, archdiocesan spokesperson Kevin Gavin, and Archbishop Chaput, but they did not respond to her, whether because they were not prepared to give her an answer or because of problems within the diocese caused by the enormous size of the CYO programs. Budd oversees forty-six football programs with thousands of children and hundreds of volunteer staff. Recent financial problems for the church have resulted in cutbacks on professional and support staffing.

Experiencing the church hierarchy as unresponsive, the Pla family decided that the next step was to garner public attention and support. Caroline's mother placed a petition on change.org, a Web site that provides a space for people to educate the public about a situation they would like to "change." People respond by signing the petition and commenting. By the time Seal Pla's petition was closed, it had 108,000 signatures. The preamble described the facts of the case, argued that the rule was "archaic," and made the moral argument that Caroline was as concerned about future players as she was about herself. Here's the text:

To:

Archdiocese of Philadelphia CYO Office,
Office of CYO Sports Kenneth A. Gavin,
Director of Communications, Archdiocese of Philadelphia
Archbishop Charles Chaput, Archbishop of Philadelphia
Leslie Davila, Archdiocese of Philadelphia

Stop Discrimination—Change the CYO Football Rule—Allow Girls to Play. It is one of the lone remaining organizations that discriminate [sic] against girls in football. The ability of a girl to be able to participate and compete safely has been proven. Girls are allowed to play Pop Warner football and even the NFL has no "male-only" rule. Caroline Pla has been fortunate enough to be part of a special CYO team the last two years, where she got to experience the camaraderie and ultimate team atmosphere of football, while representing her local CYO program. She was physically able to compete, and was a contributer [sic] and equal part of the team. According to the rule, she is no longer allowed to continue, as the CYO office looks to enforce this archaic language in their handbook—that football is for boys. The rule, as it stands now, will prevent any girl in the future from participating in and be [sic] part of a CYO football team. Moreover, because schools in the Archdiocese take federal funds, it may also be a violation of Title IX to discontinue allowing girls to play. Caroline wants more than anything that this rule be updated and modernized to reflect the times. Simply change the rule and allow girls to play.

Sincerely,

[Your name][2]

The petition also notes a legal issue, "it may also be a violation of Title IX to discontinue allowing girls to play." The awkward language is there for a reason. The director of advocacy for the Women's Sports Foundation, Nancy Hogshead-Makar, explained. Generally, if an organization accepts federal funds for any program they run (in the case of the archdiocese it would be a school lunch program), Title IX requires compliance with making equal opportunity to play sports available to girls. But there is an exemption for integration of single-sex sports. However, a legal precedent, *Mercer v. Duke University*, suggests another possibility. A court ruled that Duke University had discriminated against Heather Sue Mercer, a kicker, when they kicked her off the team, because she had been allowed to play previously. The legal reasoning would be that the CYO could not "discontinue allowing girls to play" once they had permitted them to do so. Like Mercer, Pla would have to be allowed to continue to play since she had been on the team already.[3]

Religious organizations often claim exemption from federal legislation when it comes to matters of gender and sexuality based on their First Amendment rights. Although freedom of religion permits the Catholic Church to exclude women from the priesthood, such reasoning is not often applied in legal cases to other church-sponsored activities like CYO football. Yet for many conservative Catholics permitting Pla to play is a violation of conscience. Girls should not play contact sports with boys.

The petition campaign drew the attention of Ellen DeGeneres, who tweeted encouragement and interviewed Caroline Pla on her television show. As the case began receiving national attention, Archbishop Chaput sent the Pla family an e-mail, expressing his distress that they went to the media to plead their case rather than waiting for his decision.

Chaput's decision came soon thereafter. On March 13, 2013, Chaput rejected the findings of the review panel he had constituted, which voted 16–3 against allowing Caroline Pla to play. Citing legal concerns, practices of other dioceses around the country, and the interests of coaches and parents, Chaput ruled that girls could play in 2013. He called his ruling provisional, however, and noted that it would be subject to review in the future. In the meantime, Caroline Pla (and Grace, the girl who is following in her footsteps) will be permitted to play for the Romans.

ACTIVITIES

ACTIVITY 1

Read the following statements from individual Catholics:

A

The last line of that Archdiocese statement offers some hope. It reads: "(The policy) is currently being reviewed and will be addressed moving forward to provide complete clarity." As a Catholic, I do hope that means they are going to let Caroline and other little girls who are good enough play. I am praying that the Archdiocese learns from its public relations stumbles of the past and makes the right call.

For some guidance, I direct the Archdiocese decision-makers to the words of Pla's coach, Jim Reichwein. "If you can tackle, if you can block, it has nothing to do if you are a boy or a girl, or live in a mansion or are homeless or the color of your skin. Football the game figures it out."

Football the game has already figured out that Caroline Pla can play. I just hope the Archdiocese can do the same.[4]

B

Then there is the religious aspect. This is another case of the religious right to conscience being ignored by much of society. No individual, and we mean absolutely no individual, has the right to violate the rights of the religious. Of course, that point shall be dismissed. Liberals believe they have the moral authority to force anything on anyone. That includes the religious conscience. The left is only for rights they believe exist.

We hope that the Archdiocese sticks to its guns and will not relent. But whether it does or does not, it is good that it has called attention to such matters. The question of whether girls should play contact sports with boys isn't really being considered properly. Neither is the issue of religious rights. What is it that so many people, particularly on the left, say? Open your mind when seeking answers. That doesn't seem, however, to apply to their thoughts.[5]

Create a dialogue between these two individuals. How do you imagine them continuing the conversation? Write a brief response to each of these comments that shows appreciation for the other person's point of view and also provides respectful disagreement with their perspective. Share your response with one of your classmates, who will then add an additional response for each.

ACTIVITY 2

Watch Caroline Pla's interview on *Ellen*.[6] Is there a Catholic dimension to the conversation? Should there be? What questions would you ask Caroline that would focus more on her religion, her love of football, and her case against the CYO?

ACTIVITY 3

The CYO originally cited safety as their main concern. The Women in Sports Foundation responded that boys and girls have the same safety risks in that age category. This was Caroline's response to the safety question: "A long time ago when women weren't treated equally the Archdiocese said this was for our safety," said Caroline Pla. "But they can't say that anymore. If we sign up, we know what we want and what we are getting into. And we have to get our parents permission so they also know what we are getting into."

Discussing how aware she was of the safety issue in the sport and the case of more than forty-five hundred former players who in 2014 won a settlement in their suit against the NFL in federal court that showed the league ignored and denied the link between football and brain damage, Pla added of the archdiocese, "If they want to ban girls, they have to consider banning boys too."[7]

Explain why you agree or disagree with Caroline Pla's response. Does the Catholic Church have a responsibility to speak out about safety issues in football? What should religious organizations do about balancing young people's desires to play contact sports and the known safety risks? Research the controversy over sports concussions and provide expert opinions to support your answers.

CASE 12

Should the Roman Catholic Church Condemn Bullfighting in Spain?

Fig. 12.1. A Spanish bullfight from the Ernest Hemingway Collection. Courtesy of the JFK Presidential Library Audiovisual Archives, Boston.

GOAL: To consider whether the Catholic Church has an obligation to publicly condemn bullfighting.

In 1567 Pope Pius V published a papal bull (a public notice about a vital matter of social concern), entitled *De salutis gregis dominici* ("On the Health of the Lord's Flock"), declaring bullfights to be "cruel and base spectacles of the devil and not of man," not in keeping with "Christian piety and charity," and prohibiting them in Christian lands. The consequence for a prince or official who permitted a bullfight was excommunication and denial of a Christian burial. Church officials (regular and secular) were prohibited from attending or participating in bullfights and would be punished with excommunication as well. The pope reminded his audience that although many believed a bullfight was an appropriate way to honor a saint or conduct a religious festival, it was not. The pope's statement rendered null any promises or oaths made for that purpose.[1]

If Spanish princes and ecclesiastical leaders had heeded the pope's words, the matter would be closed and there would be no need for us to consider the question of whether the Roman Catholic Church should be speaking out about bullfighting today. But the papal bull was ignored, even in the sixteenth century. The king of Spain, Phillip II, prohibited its publication in his land. Later popes mitigated the decree. In 1585 Pope Gregory XIII reiterated the ban on including bullfights in religious festivals, and also the ban on clergy participation, but removed all other prohibitions. Later, Clement VII exempted secular clergy. Spanish clergy published rejoinders supporting the traditions of bullfighting and denying that it was sinful for clergy to be spectators. Ironically, when an archbishop of Valencia in the early sixteenth century who had agreed with Pope Pius's assessment was canonized, the festival in his honor included a bullfight, or *corrida de toros*, as the sport is known in Spanish.[2]

Bullfighting is classified as a blood sport, like boxing, hunting, and dog and cock fighting, because of its violent nature. Some people don't consider bullfighting a sport because the contests do not involve competition between human actors. Ernest Hemingway famously said, "The bullfight is not a sport in the Anglo-Saxon sense of the word, that is, it is not an equal contest or an attempt at an equal contest between a bull and a man. Rather it is a tragedy."[3]

However, bullfighting resembles sports in many respects. The victor of the contest between the bull and the matador may be predetermined. But it is a contest, nonetheless, that operates under very strict rules and whose quality is judged by a designated president and also by the audience. Often bullfights are one aspect (usually the highlight) of local festivals commemorating Christian saints or important figures in the history of the town in which they take place. As such they are highly ritualized spectacles, as are most sporting contests.

Although modern bullfighting dates to the eighteenth century, its origins go back to ancient times. Many believe it began as a religious ritual, like most ancient games, but whether it had pagan or Christian origins is unknown. By the Middle Ages bullfighting was a common practice for both elites and the masses. They were often part of marriage rituals, since the bull was a symbol of sexual potency. And they were broadly associated with the canonization of saints and religious festivals.[4]

Bullfighting became a commercial spectacle in the eighteenth century, a bit ahead of the popularity of spectator sports in England and the United States. Bullrings were among the first modern stadia. The fights made money and were often held as fundraisers. Churches and other organizations used money raised from bullfights to build buildings and pay salaries. The contests were originally held on Monday afternoons, but they became a drain on the economy as people would go to bullfights instead of returning to work after siestas, and Sunday afternoon became the preferred time. Some in the Church hierarchy complained, but most accommodated, rescheduling mass so that it would not have to compete with this popular entertainment. In the mid-nineteenth century Pope Pius IX accommodated the request of the Spanish government to reduce the number of religious holidays to create more opportunities to schedule the bullfights.

Bullfighting is a topic that continues to raise passions today, particularly for supporters of animal rights who deplore any sports where animals are injured or killed like cockfighting and dogfighting. When the Atlanta

Falcon's star quarterback Michael Vick was convicted of involvement in an illegal dogfighting ring in 2007, he served twenty-one months in prison. Along with cockfighting and dogfighting, the bullfight is banned in most countries. But as of this writing there are over twenty thousand bullfights annually in Spain, Portugal, southern France, and several Latin American countries. (In Portugal the bull is not killed at the end of the contest, and therefore it is less controversial.) For our case study, we will look primarily at bullfighting in Spain where much of the outrage has been focused.

To understand the concerns of animal rights activists, it's important to describe a typical bullfight. The fight often takes place in the context of other rituals, including a traditional "running of the bulls." The event often begins with a parade into the stadium, where the -president (usually a high-ranking official who judges the contest and determines the matador's reward) waves a white handkerchief to mark that the fight is underway. There are six events. Three matadors take turns, six bulls are killed. The bulls are bred for the purpose of the *corrida*. When the first bull is released, three *banderilleros* maneuver it into position with elaborate gestures with their capes. Next, *picadores* enter on horseback to jab the bull with specially prepared spears in order to weaken its neck muscles. Although horses in the past were often gored by the bull's horns, today the horses have special garments that protect them. Next the *banderilleros* return carrying darts with colorful ribbons (*banderillas*) that they thrust into the bull's neck in order to slow it down. The matador then appears, salutes the president, and asks permission to kill the bull. He (or, in recent times, she) may also dedicate the match to someone. The matador proceeds to perform a series of passes with her red cape, designed to tire the bull while also drawing it closer. The crowd's response signals the level of their pleasure with his performance, and this audience response is taken into account by the president in determining the matador's reward. After a period of fifteen minutes, the matador then uses his sword to attempt to kill the bull. Many, but not all, succeed; some more proficiently and cleanly than others.

Each fight ends with the crowd responding to the matador with flowers, shouts, and waving handkerchiefs. The president then awards the matador a trophy (and possibly one or two ears and the tail of the bull), if she has done the kill well and cleanly, or does not if he has failed.

One need only go to the Web site of animal rights organizations like SHARK to see all the arguments (and videos) against bullfighting, or what they term "animal torture."[5] A description of the kill by a British man who lived near a bullring when he went to teach in Madrid illustrates why animal rights activists are seeking to outlaw bullfighting:

Once the matador has strutted his stuff it is time to kill the bull. If the bull is to die quickly, the sword must be plunged with the proper force and in the perfect direction into an area of the neck the size of a bottle cap. It rarely happens. Most of the time the bull is gutted internally. The "experts" watch the colour of the blood pouring from the mouth of the animal and offer their educated guesses as to what is actually happening inside: did the sword enter the lungs? Was the aorta penetrated? Is he drowning in his own blood? At this point men with capes do all they can to force the bull to move so they can insure the destruction of the internal organs by the misplaced sword so the matador will look like a better killer. Sometimes the bull will collapse after a while. If death—as it often happens—still does not follow, eventually someone severs the spinal medulla with a special instrument and the bull finally dies.[6]

It is a common practice of animal rights organizations to appeal to the Church to condemn bullfighting, and contacting the Church is the one thing that is universally recommended. Spain is a predominantly Catholic nation (culturally, 90 percent of Spaniards identify as Catholic and 50 percent attend church regularly), and a strong condemnation by the pope might have powerful impact. Movie star and sex symbol Brigitte Bardot made headlines with her request to John Paul II in 2000. Bullfighting was first condemned by a pope, and other popes (among them Pius IX and Benedict XV) have spoken out against it. The current pope, Francis, presumably took his name from St. Francis of Assisi, known for his kindness to animals, and animal rights activists are hoping that he will condemn bullfighting. (It is banned by law in his native Argentina.) They also see a moral imperative they believe the Church cannot ignore: "The cruel torture of these animals represents an attitude of abuse towards nature and the oppressed that is not acceptable as a part of religion. How much time do we need in order to see that God did not put everything on the earth for us to rape and plunder?"[7]

But bullfighting's close association with Catholicism in Spain also makes it difficult for the Church, as Church leaders don't want to alienate the Spaniards, many of whom see no moral problem with *corridas*. They point out that more people are injured in other sports (boxing, football, soccer to name a few.) Bullfighting is a major aspect of Spain's economy. The industry itself employs many people, breeding is a major aspect of animal husbandry, and it is a significant dimension of tourism. *Corridas* are also deeply associated with Spanish culture and tradition, and criticisms from outside raise questions about negative (particularly European) racial attitudes toward Spain. Bullfighting is also an art, and matadors are skillful at what they do, which is what the audience appreciates.

Spanish clergy also have supported *corridas,* as described by Kenneth Tynan: "You will see priests down at the corrals every morning. . . . It is hard to conceive of a Protestant clergyman at a *corrida.* I watched two priests in the square demonstrating to a group of Vassar girls the correct use of the cape and *banderillas* they bought as souvenirs: the magenta folds swung softly while the father pivoted, following with his eyes the trajectory of his imagined bull."[8]

Many Spanish churches raise money through bullfights and have also been involved in breeding. While they don't authorize bullfights during religious festivals, they certainly permit them to take place. Pope John Paul II accepted the matador's cape on more than one occasion.[9]

Ernest Hemingway, whose photograph of bullfighting begins this chapter, is also responsible for the focus on Catholicism. His exhaustive nonfiction study of Spanish bullfighting, *Death in the Afternoon*, examined the contests in Madrid and Pamplona, Spain where he had set his earlier work, *The Sun Also Rises.* Like many Spanish bullfights, this one originated in association with the calendar of Christian saints. It is part of an annual festival in honor of San Fermin, a third-century Christian martyr and the patron saint of Navarre. The festival dates back to the end of the six-teenth century, about the time of Pius's bull. (As I write, on July 12, 2013, three young men were sent to the hospital gored and seriously injured during the running of the bulls in Pamplona. Another twenty-three were injured the following day.)

In *Death in the Afternoon* Hemingway grappled with the moral and reli-gious dimensions of the *corrida*:

> He [the matador] must have a spiritual enjoyment of the moment of killing. Killing cleanly and in a way which gives you aesthetic pleasure and pride has always been one of the greatest enjoyments of a part of the human race. * * * Once you accept the rule of death thou shalt not kill is an easily and naturally obeyed commandment. But when a man is still in rebellion against death he has pleasure in taking to himself one of the Godlike attributes, that of giving it. This is one of the most profound feelings in those men who enjoy killing. These things are done in pride and pride, of course, is a Christian sin and a pagan virtue. But it is pride which makes the bull-fight and true enjoyment of killing which makes the great matador.[10]

Although killing is a Christian sin, the Catholic Church holds humans to be of higher moral value than animals. The 1567 papal bull "On the Health of the Lord's Flock" was centrally focused on God's *human* flock. Humans are made in the image of God, according to traditional Catholic teaching, but animals are not. Animals do not have as high a moral status because they are not creatures who reason. While animals are certainly God's creatures and should not be mistreated, the fight for animal rights is not a high priority for the Roman Catholic Church. John Paul II made this clear when he responded to a request from one activist to intercede to end bullfighting: "The holy father appreciates the efforts being made to secure proper treatment of animals, and as you know, he has himself on various occasions urged such respect. The defence of all living creatures, of course, has to be seen in the context of the principal duty of protecting human beings, created in the image and likeness of God, from the crimes of abortion, euthanasia and sexual abuse and from other attacks on their dignity and worth."[11]

ACTIVITIES

ACTIVITY 1

Write a letter to the pope explaining why you think he should speak out against bullfighting. Be sure to include at least three arguments to persuade him. Also include three reasons why he might say no and argue against them.

ACTIVITY 2

Write a letter to PETA (People for the Ethical Treatment of Animals) explaining why you think bullfighting should be respected. Make sure at least one argument comes from a religious perspective engaging their pleas to the Vatican.

ACTIVITY 3

Using the literature about sport as religion, make an argument for whether or not you see bullfighting as a religion. Use Smart's criteria and examples from the texts in this case study.

CASE 13

The Florida State University Seminoles' Osceola and Renegade

MASCOTS OR SYMBOLS?

Fig. 13.1. Florida State Chief Osceola and Renegade during a game against Wake Forest at Doak Cambell Stadium on Sept. 15, 2012. AP Photo/Don Juan Moore.

GOAL: To examine the use of Native American symbols and imagery by sports teams in North America.

High school, college, and professional teams use team names, logos, songs, chants, and iconic images (usually known as mascots) to shape and express their identity. These images are largely imaginative representations tied to some value the school or city is associated with, from the whimsical (Syracuse's Otto the Orangeman) to the violent (Vikings or Trojans). These mascots are often animals to symbolize courage or perseverance (Lions, Tigers, and Bears), sometimes imaginative creatures (Phanatics, Pirates, or Billikens), or based on something related to the school or municipality's history or economy (like the Green Bay Packers or Pittsburgh Steelers). In a few cases teams use religious iconography—Knights, Saints, and Devils are common examples, not to mention the Quakers of the University of Pennsylvania. But ethnic groups (with the exception of Notre Dame's Fighting Irish) are not generally considered appropriate—there are no teams called African Americans, even at historically black colleges. The exception is Native Americans and their iconography, both religious and ethnic, which accounts for thousands of these symbolic representations. This anomaly is still a contentious matter in the world of sports. Although many high school and university teams have changed their names and mascots in response to concerns that have been raised about this stereotyping for the past thirty years, many have not. And while some professional teams have made minor adjustments, the Washington football team is still the Redskins and the Cleveland Indians' mascot is still a grinning caricature.

Unlike some of our other cases, which are primarily studied by scholars of religion, Native American mascots have been discussed and analyzed by sports scholars in law, sociology, education, and race and ethnic studies, as illustrated by the extensive resource list for this case. Looking at the issue from the perspective of religion and sport adds to this conversation in several respects. Although Native Americans do not use the term *religion* to describe their way of life, scholars of religion include indigenous traditions in our studies. We are curious about how North American tribal groups understand the sacred and the values they live by, the rituals they perform, the objects, music, and dance they use in ceremonies—in other words the elements of Native culture that bear a strong family resemblance to other religions. We are also interested in the ways in which other religions, mostly Christianity and New Age spirituality, have interacted with Native American life. We seek to understand both the harm done by religious seekers, missionaries, and educators and also to document how Native individuals and groups like the Native American Church have embraced and adapted Christianity, and how Native traditions have been borrowed and changed by spiritual seekers. There is no doubt that the Native mascots, team names, chants, and displays in the world of sports borrow from sacred traditions, and as religion scholars we want to understand this phenomenon.

The mascots and rituals are part of this conversation about religion and sports not only because they correspond to or have been borrowed from Native sacred traditions but also because they have been transformed in the process into a critical aspect of the religion of sports, especially in college settings. While it is often suggested that mascots, pep rallies, songs, and chants are trivial, it is obvious (and will be well demonstrated through our case study) that they perform the function of venerated objects, powerful symbols, and community-creating rituals that convey deep meaning to those who participate in sports culture.

Who "owns" these religious symbols, and what does their use convey? We will look at the case of the Florida State University (FSU) Seminoles, who have gained legal rights to the name that belongs to the Seminole tribes of Florida and Oklahoma as well as tribal permission to use their name and image in the FSU logo, commercial products, and ritual celebrations.

In 1947 the Florida state legislature changed the name of the Florida State College for Women in Tallahassee to Florida State University and returned it to its former status as a coeducational public institution to accommodate the large number of male World War II veterans going back to school under the GI Bill. The university began to build a strong program of intercollegiate athletics. The students were given the opportunity to vote on their mascot, and they chose Seminoles. Although live mascot actors were not yet in vogue, the student newspaper adopted a logo with the head of a Seminole in profile, wearing a feathered headdress, face paint, and a serious expression. The logo was redesigned in 1965 as an animated "Savage Sam," dancing, sporting feathers, and carrying an ax. A few years later that logo was replaced by the profiled Seminole image that remains on the FSU Web site today.[1]

Seminole is the term used by Europeans for all the Native tribes in Florida (from the Spanish word, *cimarrón,* "wild"), although it originally referred to a specific subgroup in North Florida that had been part of the Creek tribes. When Spain ceded Florida to the United States in 1819, President Andrew Jackson began a campaign to relocate the indigenous population to "Indian Territory" (Oklahoma). Some moved voluntarily. Many others resisted, resulting in the protracted Seminole Wars. By 1842 most of the Seminoles had been removed as prisoners of war, although a small number remained. One of the leaders of the resistance was Osceola (1804–1838). Osceola was not a hereditary chief and was probably of mixed European and Creek ancestry. He rose to prominence as an outspoken critic of the removal policy and became a military leader during the Second Seminole War. Osceola led a truce party to talks with the U.S. commander, and although they came in peace they were captured and imprisoned. He died in prison soon thereafter, presumably of malaria. He was decapitated, his body buried, and his head taken to New York where it was later displayed in a museum. His brave leadership and dishonorable capture drew public attention (from whites and Indians alike) and made him a martyr. The last remaining Seminoles continued armed resistance, and all but a few hundred were finally removed to Oklahoma by 1858.

The Oklahoma Seminoles became U.S. citizens in 1901 and reestablished their tribal government in 1935. The small number of Seminoles who remained in Florida reestablished relationships with the U.S. government and became a federally recognized tribe in 1957, incorporated as the Seminole Tribe of Florida (STF). They live on six reservations and were the first tribe to become involved in the gaming industry, from which they continue to derive their income. Since 2011 the tribe has been led by Chief Jim Billie, who had previously served in the role from 1979–2001, but left amid accusations of fiscal corruption.

Florida State University developed a relationship with the STF in the 1970s when one of the mascots they created in the 1960s for their basketball team, Chief Fullabull, came under attack from American Indian students and some STF members. They were deeply distressed by the antics of Chief Fullabull (not to mention his name), a student who engaged in half-time clowning and other entertainment. At this time other colleges and universities began changing their mascots, names, and logos in response to full-scale protests by the American Indian Movement and their supporters. The Stanford Indians became the Cardinal in 1972, and many other schools similarly abandoned their mascots and changed their names and logos out of respect.

The student who portrayed Chief Fullabull tried to satisfy their complaints by changing his name to Chief Wampumstompum. Eventually the mascot was renamed Yahola and stopped the routines that were derived from Hollywood and Wild West shows, which depicted Indians either as violent savages in war paint or scantily clad buffoons. The football mascot, Sammy Seminole, was invented in 1958 and derived from that tradition. Sammy was also played by a student wearing a breechcloth and single feather. He led chants and did a variety of cheerleading and acrobatic stunts, barefoot. Although Sammy was officially removed in 1968, there is evidence that he made reappearances during the 1970s and was the main subject of the dialogue between leaders of FSU and the STF.

In 1978 a new mascot was introduced, Chief Osceola and his horse, an appaloosa named Renegade. According to the FSU administration, the STF was consulted concerning the creation of his costume and gestures, but apparently not his name, since Osceola never achieved the status of chief, and there is no record of the name of his horse, which was also not likely to have been an appaloosa.

Like his predecessors, this mascot is played by an FSU student who receives scholarship money for this task. Only one student at a time performs as the chief, and so far all the students have been of European ancestry. The student does two years of apprenticeship and training before performing at games. He must have good grades, strong equestrian skills, and good moral character to be considered for the role. The horse and rider mascot performance was invented by an alumnus of FSU, Bill Durham, with support from the wife of the football coach, Ann Bowden. Durham (and now his son Allen) selects and trains the student performers, provides the horses, and choreographs and coaches the elaborate performance. Coach Bowden also supports the use of this imagery.

At every home football game since September 1978, the same ritualized performance has been enacted. Before the teams enter, the student, dressed in bandana, fringed shirt, pants, and boots in the school colors of garnet and gold, and wearing face paint, rides into Doak Campbell Stadium bareback on an appaloosa named Renegade. He carries a twenty-eight pound flaming spear festooned with feathers, also in the school colors, that he holds high in the air. The outfit is authentic, but the appaloosa, war paint, and spear are not Seminole traditions. Horse and rider wait under the goal posts as the teams enter the field behind the corps of cheerleaders holding huge banners with the school logo and team name. The FSU band, the Marching Chiefs, leads the crowd in the "War Chant." The chanting ritual developed in 1984 when fans began to sing along with the band and make an accompanying gesture that has been widely copied by other teams with Native names and logos. It is known widely as "the tomahawk chop." On the Web site of the booster club the following explanation is given: "who knew that a few years later the gesture would be picked up by other team's [sic] fans and named the 'tomahawk chop?' It's a term we did not choose and officially do not use. Our university's goal is to be a model community that treats all cultures with dignity while celebrating diversity. I have appointed a task force to review our use of Seminole Indian symbols and traditions."[2]

After the teams enter the playing field, Renegade raises up on his hind legs, and horse and rider trot to midfield where Osceola plants the flaming arrow and rides off to the other side. He sits on the horse during the national anthem and stays in character, remaining still and silent; he is forbidden from speaking or cheering or walking. All of this can be observed on the Internet; I stopped counting at five hundred homemade versions posted on YouTube.

The U.S. Commission on Civil Rights issued a statement in 2001 condemning the use of Native team names and mascots in public institutions, and many other organizations, from the NAACP to the American Psychological Association to various church bodies, have done so as well. In 2005 the National Collegiate Athletic Association (NCAA) made a ruling that schools with Indian mascots, logos, and nicknames deemed "hostile and abusive" would be required to change them or face penalties. They would no longer be invited to host postseason games in any sport except for football, over which the NCAA had no control. They would not be able to bring mascots or wear uniforms with offensive logos to any postseason tournament. The NCAA listed eighteen schools, including Florida State, that would be asked to change their practices. The NCAA had previously recommended that schools make these changes, but this was the first time they included sanctions.

Florida State's president, T. K. Wetherell, responded by threatening legal action. He told the press that the NCAA's assertion about FSU was due simply to their ignorance of the close relationship between the school and the Florida Seminole Tribe. Florida governor Jeb Bush condemned the NCAA's stance as "politically correct" and also chided the NCAA ruling as a misunderstanding of local culture. Republican state senator Jim King, who had proposed legislation in 1999 requiring Florida State to make Osceola and Renegade their legal mascots, said that he would submit the legislation again.

The NCAA permitted schools to appeal the ruling. Of the eighteen schools cited, fourteen changed their names or mascots. Florida State appealed and was granted a waiver by the NCAA. Their argument was based on testimony from the leaders of the Florida Seminoles, who reiterated their position that the FSU imagery was not demeaning or insulting in any way and that they were fully in support of the school's policies. Because the NCAA representative claimed they made the ruling based on complaints from Oklahoma Seminoles, FSU also presented evidence from their official council that they had no objection.

David Narconey, a Florida Seminole and member of the American Indian Movement, represented another point of view. He found Florida State's representations of Seminoles harmful and degrading and argued that many other Seminoles disagree with their leadership. He pointed out that the Oklahoma Seminoles had signed on to a statement condemning Native mascots several years before. He also raised concerns about what the Florida Tribe was getting in return for their assent. Their gaming industry depends on the support of the Florida legislature, which includes many men and women like Jim King who are FSU alumni. Florida State pointed out that they support the tribe by providing scholarships to Seminoles, but there are generally fewer than ten Seminole Indians attending the university at any given time. The university also honors tribal leaders, including them in homecoming events and commencement ceremonies. To Narconey, these efforts do not add up to a strong relationship. He claims that for FSU sales and licensing of these images is a multimillion-dollar business and he has not seen evidence that the tribe receives any portion of those proceeds.

The NCAA granted the exemption based on the premise that the Native American Seminoles owned their image and therefore the right to determine its use. It is based on an understanding of culture as property that belongs exclusively to one group, rather than something that changes, crosses cultures, and is forever being borrowed and reshaped in other contexts—sometimes respectfully and sometimes not.

The authentic dress and the representation of an important figure in Seminole history are the evidence on which the property argument is based. The ritual of Osceola and Renegade also reflects the ritual culture of Florida State. The traditional Seminole and Creek cultures were matrilineal and tended to be peaceful. According to some scholars, the emphasis on the accoutrements of war (spears, face paint, horses, and chants) is not in keeping with the predominant ethos of Seminole culture. But it fits well with a college football culture that values bravery, perseverance, showmanship, and victory. Using these criteria, it could be argued that FSU, like the practitioners of New Age spirituality, have borrowed elements from native culture to create religious rituals of their own.

Florida State leaders counter with the argument that their whole purpose is to honor the heritage of the Florida Seminoles and their example of bravery and perseverance, fighting against U.S. tyranny and refusing to surrender or be moved from their homes. They see using these images as an opportunity to educate students and the general public about Native

American history and culture. Americans would never know about Osceola's rebellion if not for the attention of collegiate football. While some Native mascots might be inappropriate, they should not all be lumped together as if there were one Native American tradition. They do not use the term *mascot* for Osceola and Renegade, but refer to them as symbols. The FSU depiction of Seminoles is specific, unique, and meant to accord respect. In 2012 the FSU administration added a cartoon horse named Cimarron, the word that is the linguistic origin of the Spanish term that became the English Seminole. Cimarron is a mascot, not a symbol; a figure appropriate for less dignified occasions when some representation of the university was needed, particularly for children's events, to protect the dignity of Osceola and Renegade.

The case has received copious attention from scholars, who almost universally argue that the Osceola and Renegade ritual is inauthentic, stereotypical, and demeans Native Americans. They argue that Native American mascots and team names should be categorized as IIED (intentional infliction of emotional distress) and subject to litigation for hostile environment harassment. In other states legal remedies such as theft of trademark suits or legislative bans are possible, and pressure for them continues, but with the support of the Florida legislature and the Seminole Tribe of Florida they can't use legal means to express their opinions. Scholars have argued that polls, like the one in *Sports Illustrated* in 2002,[3] suggest that the majority of Americans (Indian and non) do not find Chief Osceola offensive. And they question the legitimacy of polls like ESPN's 2011 "Traditions" contest, which named the Florida State pregame ritual the best in the nation.[4] But that sociological data remains and points to the fact that scholars aren't always in sync with popular opinion.

ACTIVITY

You attend the University of Minnesota. Leaders of the student body are convinced that using Native Americans mascots and images is wrong. They were impressed with decisions by the University of Wisconsin and the University of Iowa not to play nonconference games against teams with mascots and want to convince university officials to cancel an upcoming athletic event against Florida State University as a protest. The student body is being asked to vote in a referendum on whether they support this position. Half the class will form teams to support canceling the event and the other half will oppose it. You will be randomly assigned to a group. Your task will be to design a campaign to support your point. You may choose to write newspaper editorials, design a Web site, create a polling mechanism, or challenge the other side to a debate.

Disclaimer

It is important to me as a teacher not to make my feelings or opinions about the topics we discuss known to my students. My goal, in this text as in my classroom, is to present cases, supported by a variety of scholarly views about them that include well-reasoned disagreements from many angles. I encourage students to develop their own positions in response, often supplemented by their own research, and then form opinions that can be supported by evidence and argument. But when discussing this case, I admit to a bias. I believe that using Native American imagery in sport is wrong and should be ended, although I am ambivalent about the means that should be used to bring about this change.

Although I share this opinion with many scholars and legal analysts who have written about this issue, it is clear that there are a variety of responsible positions that are in disagreement, and I have made every effort to present those positions respectfully and describe this case neutrally. My own position is based primarily on my life experience. I grew up in the 1950s when playing Cowboys and Indians was common and unremarkable. Most of the television shows I watched as a child on Saturday mornings were Westerns where there were some good Indians (like Tonto, the loyal sidekick), but mostly bad Indians (the violent savages). Dressing in feathered headdresses and war paint for daily play, not to mention Halloween, was common practice. Although I've come to understand as an adult that "playing Indian" may have been an ingenious strategy for white America to cope psychologically with the genocide that our government committed, it did not expunge my guilt over being part of a settler colonialist nation; in fact, it exacerbated it. So I am incapable of viewing with total neutrality any expression that appears to me to participate in the diminishment of Native culture and tradition. Nonetheless, I chose this case because I believe Florida State's position is both honest and thoughtful and so this case provides a real opportunity to think through this dilemma.

RESOURCES

Black, Jason Edward. "The 'Mascotting' of Native America: Construction, Commodity, and Assimilation." *American Indian Quarterly* 26.4 (Autumn 2002): 605–622.

Bloom, John and Randy Hanson. "Warriors and Thieves: Appropriation of the Warrior Motif in Representations of Native American Athletes." In John Bloom and Michael Nevin Willard, eds., *Sports Matters: Race, Recreation and Culture,* 246–263. New York: New York University Press, 2002.

Bresnahan, Mary Jiang and Kelly Flowers. "The Effects of Involvement in Sports on Attitudes Toward Native American Sports Mascots." *Howard Journal of Communications* 19 (2008): 165–181.

Brown, Kristine A. "Native American Team Names and Mascots: Disparaging and Insensitive or Just a Part of the Game?" *Sports Lawyers Journal* 9 (2002): 115–130.

Cummings, André Douglas Pond. "Progress Realized? The Continuing American Indian Mascot Quandary." *Marquette Sports Law Review* 18.2 (2008): 309–335.

Farnell, Brenda. "The Fancy Dance of Racializing Discourse." *Journal of Sport and Social Issues* 28.1 (February 2004): 30–55.

Finkelstein, Jason. "What the Sioux Should Do: Lanham Act Challenges in the Post-Harjo Era." *Cardozo Arts and Entertainment Law Journal* 26 (2008–2009): 301–334.

Ford, James B. *Seminole Mascot: Osceola, the Seminole Tribe, and Their Celebration by Florida State University.* Privately published, 2012.

George, Glenn. "Playing Cowboys and Indians." *Virginia Sports and Entertainment Law Journal* 6.1 (Fall 2006): 90–123.

Goldstein, Aaron. "Intentional Infliction of Emotional Distress: Another Attempt at Eliminating Native American Mascots." *Journal of Gender, Race, and Justice* 3 (2000): 689–713.

King, C. Richard. "This Is Not an Indian: Situating Claims About Indianness in Sporting Worlds." *Journal of Sport and Social Issues* 28.1 (February 2004): 3–10.

——, ed. *The Native American Mascot Controversy: A Handbook.* Lanham, MD: Scarecrow Press, 2010.

———, Ellen J. Staurowsky, Lawrence Baca, Laurel R. Davis, and Cornel Pewewardy. "Of Polls and Race Prejudice: *Sports Illustrated*'s Errant 'Indian Wars.'" *Journal of Sport and Social Issues* 26.4 (November 2002): 381–402.

Mezey, Naomi. "The Paradoxes of Cultural Property." 107 *Columbia Law Review* 2004–2046 (2007).

Remillard, Arthur J. "Holy War on the Football Field: Religion and the Florida State University Indian Mascot Controversy." In James Vlasich, ed., *Horsehide, Pigskin, Oval Tracks, and Apple Pie: Essays on Sports and American Culture*, 104–118. Jefferson, NC: McFarland, 2005.

Spindel, Carol. *Dancing at Halftime: Sports and the Controversy Over American Indian Mascots.* New York: New York University Press, 2000.

Staurowsky, Ellen. "Privilege at Play: On the Legal and Social Fictions That Sustain American Indian Sport Imagery." *Journal of Sports and Social Issues* 28.1 (February 2004): 11–29.

———, "'You Know, We Are All Indian': Exploring White Power and Privilege in Reactions to the NCAA Native American Mascot Policy." *Journal of Sport and Social Issues* 31.1 (February 2007): 61–76.

Taylor, Michael. "The Salamanca Warriors: A Case Study of an 'Exception to the Rule.'" *Journal of Anthropological Research* 67 (2011): 245–265.

CASE 14

Jack Taylor's 138 Points

IS "RUNNING UP THE SCORE" CHRISTIAN?

Fig. 14.1. Jack Taylor. Cory Hall/Cory Hall Photography.

GOAL: to determine whether a "blowout" is morally wrong from a Christian perspective.

On November 20, 2012, Jack Taylor, a sophomore guard on the Division III Grinnell College basketball team scored 138 points. He broke the National Collegiate Athletic Association (NCAA) record set by Bevo Francis who scored 113 points for Rio Grande College in 1954. That season Frank Selvy of Furman College also scored 100 points, setting a new record in a Division I game. The professional record belongs to Wilt Chamberlain, who scored 100 points for the Philadelphia Warriors in 1962. Kobe Bryant's 81 points for the Los Angeles Lakers in 2006 is the only scoring feat that has come close.

Taylor's record was widely celebrated. In the age of social media, he trended on Twitter, drawing the admiration and attention of NBA greats Kobe Bryant, Kevin Durant, and LeBron James, who gave him the nickname "Sir Jack." Clips from the game went viral on the Web. Taylor was interviewed on *Good Morning America, NPR,* and *Jimmy Kimmel,* and the story made front page news in every media outlet. U.S. Representative Bruce Braley from Iowa entered the accomplishment into the Congressional Record. News reports discussed Taylor's background growing up in Black River Falls, Wisconsin, admiring Kobe Bryant, and transferring to Grinnell as a twenty-two year old after sustaining knee injuries at another Division III program, University of Wisconsin La Crosse. The accounts also often mentioned that Taylor went to classes the next day—Calculus and Introduction to Christianity. When interviewed, Taylor described an experience of being "in the zone."

On the Web site of the Fellowship of Christian Athletes (FCA), his feat was interpreted in a different light. An article entitled "Higher Score: Taylor Aims to Glorify Christ" discussed the event's religious meaning. Taylor's injury was responsible not only for his transfer to Grinnell but also for his conversion to Christianity and membership in FCA. On their Web site Taylor described his fame as an opportunity to praise God and not his own abilities: "'If I had scored 138 points before God saved me, it would have been a disaster. I would have turned myself into a 'god' that people could idolize. Instead, God has made me a new creation who cares more about making Jesus' name famous rather than my own.'" He credited his teammates for their unselfishness, which he also described as a Christian value: "'As a Christian . . . it isn't about you . . . it's about Jesus' righteousness. It's all about Jesus.'"

The article also focused on the prayer service Taylor had participated in before the game. The Bible text was Matthew 25. The passage, known as "The Parable of the Talents," is about learning how to make the most of your abilities. Taylor described praying for the strength to use his abilities to glorify God and concluded: "He definitely multiplied my talents that night. His fingerprints were all over that game."

In keeping with the doctrine of muscular Christianity, Taylor described what it meant to be a man. Based on Jesus's example, a man is someone who takes responsibility, who puts away "childish things" like drinking beer or getting girls. Despite his busy schedule of classes and practice, he named his primary aim as encouraging other athletes to "come and learn about Jesus" at FCA. He noted the strategic role FCA played in helping him avoid the temptation to make basketball or his own abilities into a false god. Instead, Taylor saw this moment as an opportunity to praise God in keeping with the words of (not coincidentally) Psalm 138, "I will give You thanks with all my heart; I will sing Your praise before the heavenly beings," which was posted in its entirety on the FCA Web site.[1]

The losing team also interpreted the game through a religious lens. Faith Baptist Bible College (FBBC) in Ankey, Iowa, was not affiliated with the NCAA but with the NCCAA—the National Christian College Athletic Association, in their Division II. The NCCAA was created, according to their Web site, to: "provide a Christian-based organization that functions uniquely as a national and international agency for the promotion of outreach and ministry and for the maintenance, enhancement and promotion of intercollegiate athletic competition with a Christian perspective." This means that the goal of the athletic programs is to strengthen character more than to win. As is common in the language of muscular Christian organizations, sports are where young people learn "discipline, team work, leadership, and mutual respect." Coaches must pledge to make sports a safe environment based on honesty and respect and free from commercialization and personal gain. Student athletes must also pledge to rely on God, be honest and respect authority, and celebrate gender and cultural diversity.[2]

The FBBC Web site did not feature Taylor, but focused on their star of the game, David Larson, who scored 70 points, shooting 34 of 44 layups, and the student body that was proud of their team for appearing on the national news. The coach, Brian Fincham, expressed admiration for Taylor, but also enormous pride in his team for their effort and hustle until the end of the game. Although they did double-team Taylor, in keeping with their values, they did not commit cheap fouls to try to stop him. He said the team accepted the game with Grinnell knowing that they would likely not win. As a small college with only ten players, they used games like this, which for them counted as an exhibition, as an opportunity to try things out and prepare for the season. Fincham, and the athletes, had no regrets.[3] For Tyler Betz, the team's leading scorer, this was an opportunity to practice humility, referencing Philippians 2 where Jesus submits to God. Another player, Jon Rocha, appreciated the chance to play David to Grinnell's Goliath.[4]

Apart from their similar locations in Iowa, Grinnell College is quite different from FBBC. It does have religious roots, although it is now a well-endowed secular liberal arts college. It was founded in 1846 by the Puritan-based Congregationalist denomination today known as the United Church of Christ (UCC) and is associated with liberal positions on civil, women's, and gay rights. Although Grinnell is a secular institution, it has a reputation for espousing values compatible with its liberal Protestant roots, especially social responsibility. It carries with pride the name of the abolitionist Josiah Bushnell Grinnell, and the alumni who were part of FDR's New Deal brain trust are featured prominently in their public relations efforts. More of their alumni join the Peace Corps than any other college or university because of their unique "5th year travel-service program." Their mission statement includes the goal "to graduate men and women . . . who are prepared in life and work to use their knowledge and their abilities to serve the common good."[5]

Despite Taylor's professed evangelical values and a school that comes from a liberal Protestant tradition, critics have labeled Taylor's accomplishment as exemplifying the antithesis of religious values in Christianity and in sport. The "friendly atheist" Web site gloated at the irony: "One of the more interesting aspects of his record-breaking game is the fact that his team beat Faith Bible Baptist college along the way. It's a school so religious, its website is faith.edu. . . . You have to wonder where God is when the team with "Bible" in its name loses—in spectacular fashion—to a college once ranked among the least religious schools in the country."[6]

Grinnell was pictured as a Goliath to FBBC's David in terms of the size of the student body (1,600 to 300) and their financial status (both endowment and tuition). Although both schools play Division III–style sports, the difference between the quality of play in the NCAA and the NCCAA is vast, so this was not a fair contest. One columnist compared Grinnell to Penn State as a location that proved "athletics can corrupt at all levels of competition."[7]

Taylor, as an individual player, was criticized as a ball hog, a bad role model for children, a glutton, and a selfish player because he had no assists. He took 108 shots to make 138 points—not even an impressive percentage. That his success upholds Christian values is belied, according to Amy Laura Hall, professor at Duke Divinity School, "by the unapologetic, brazen appeal to 'Jesus' right alongside the unrepentant quest to make a name for the school, the team and the player."[8]

Critics also pointed to the questionable practice of record breaking as an end in itself or a way to garner media attention. Breaking a record should not be a goal of sports contests because it changes the nature of the game. Some critics even suggested that aiming to break a record divests the record of value. If breaking a record causes embarrassment (or, as some would have it, public humiliation) to the opponent, it is wrong and contradicts Grinnell's mission of caring for society.

In an effort to break the record, the Grinnell Pioneers indulged in a "blowout;" the unsportsmanlike activity known as "running up the score." Some writers argued that, once it is clear a team is going to win (and that was the case by halftime in this contest), the winning team has an obligation to play conservatively, slow down the game, or put in the bench players. Another writer invoked Matthew 7:12 and the Golden Rule.[9] And a rabbi suggested:

> As a general rule, no team is ethically permitted to run up the score intentionally, because it demeans and belittles their opponents. In fact, the Bible provides numerous examples of legislation that promotes compassion for others that can be applied to this situation. My favorite example is the obligation to assist a person in unloading a burden off of their animal. The animal is in pain and the Bible requires us to lift the burden off its back. Our sages point out that if we are required to act compassionately towards animals, then certainly we are required to show great compassion to humans; to pick them up when they fall down and lift the burdens off their backs.[10]

To these critics running up the score goes against religious values and conforms to the worst American values that define greed and excess as good.

Other criticism was leveled not at Taylor, or Grinnell, but at the "system" that David Arseneault, who coaches the Pioneers along with his son, David Jr., invented. Arseneault was accused of corrupting Taylor by turning him into a mercenary. Taylor was the designated shooter in a "gimmicky" strategy that makes a mockery of the game of basketball; Arseneault is a charlatan.

According to Arseneault, he invented this strategy when he came to coach at Grinnell in the 1990s and discovered a highly competitive group of students who were deeply demoralized by losing. In response, he thought he'd try something unconventional. He came up with a formula for success that he described with the shorthand: "94S + 47 3's + 33%OR + 25SD + 32 TO's = W." The formula predicts that if the team takes ninety-four shots, at least forty-seven of which are three pointers, rebounds at least a third of them, takes twenty-five more shots than the other team, and makes them commit thirty-two turnovers, they are almost sure to win. To maximize the options for three-point shooting, one player is designated to take most of the shots and does not go down the court to defend. The other players also focus their defense on half-court pressure designed to create steals. The other team may get easy layup shots, but threes will always beat twos. The team carries twenty players, and they rotate in and out (like changing lines in hockey), creating a chaotic atmosphere.[11]

The Pioneers play variations on the system in every game. Taylor's teammate, Griffin Lentsch, scored a record 89 points in a game the year before and the team averages 112 points a game. To its detractors, this is a "shoot-a-palooza" and a sham. Arseneault is accused of using the system primarily to sell videos and books about it and as a way of garnering publicity for Grinnell. But to its defenders Arsenault has created an "innovative data-driven system that relies on selfless teamwork to create . . . fun basketball."[12]

Many sports writers and Internet commentators came to the Pioneers' defense. Arsenault designated Taylor that night because the new transfer had gotten off to a slow start and needed a boost to his confidence. Taylor may have taken a lot of shots, but he made the points legitimately, including twenty-seven three-pointers. There is nothing unorthodox about giving the ball to the best shooter. If a player is "in the zone," they should be given an opportunity to continue.

In defense of Grinnell, this is a Division III team. No athlete has a scholarship, and no academic standards are lowered to bring talented players onto the team. The system creates camaraderie among an unusually large number of players who are forced to play unselfishly in order to carry out the system. And Taylor was not the regular star; other players had a chance to be designated shooters. (In the next game, despite the extensive media attention, Taylor barely scored. Several games later he broke his wrist and was out for the season.)

Although Grinnell and FBBC were not evenly matched institutions, they did agree to play one another, and the FBBC coach knew about Grinnell's system and what they would be up against. Faith Baptist is a legitimate team; they were not paid off; and all the rules of basketball were observed. No one fouled deliberately or behaved discourteously. Not only did the players treat each other with respect, but Grinnell fans sincerely cheered David Larson's layups.

Running up the score is a contested issue in sports ethics. According to Nicholas Dixon, it is not necessarily unsportsmanlike. From this perspective, holding back and not playing to their best ability is more disrespectful to the other team. We can't blame athletes for not living up to their potential, and then criticize them when they give their all. Dixon suggests that arguments against running up the score are predicated on two false assumptions. The first is that the only goal of playing is winning. The second is that suffering a lopsided defeat is humiliating to the losers rather than simply an indication of different abilities or even a different performance on one particular day. If losers do experience humiliation, however, Dixon would find running up the score objectionable.[13]

On the other hand, Randolph Feezel argues that respect is not only for opponents, but also for the integrity and tradition of the game itself. Feezel argues that although running up the score is wrong and unsporting, there might be circumstances where it is justifiable. A question raised by this case is whether breaking a record would be considered one of those circumstances.[14]

In a forum on the topic on the ESPN Web site, Patrick Hruby questioned the premise that sports have a moral significance. If a game is just a game and not "quasi-sacred," then sports don't "teach any particular life lessons that can't be learned by, well, living." Johnette Howard, on the other hand, commented that there are life lessons in sports and that all routs are not created equal. She mentions Joe Louis's victory over Max Schmeling as a rout that delivered an important message. That the African American Louis decisively walloped the German, who was being touted by the Nazis as an example of racial superiority, was a moral victory. But she opposes teams treating each other disrespectfully: "who needs the Bully Rout, which is what the UConn women's basketball team did to Holy Cross in a 117–37 trouncing Monday night in another tedious expression of its remorseless quest for excellence that treats opponents like nameless, faceless foes rather than—you know—real human beings."[15]

Jack Taylor's 138-point record was both exciting and troubling. If you are conflicted about it, the activities below may help sort things out.

ACTIVITIES

ACTIVITY 1

Turn off the sound and watch the full game.[16] With a partner, record or create a transcript of your own play by play. Be sure to highlight the issues raised in the case.

ACTIVITY 2

Write a response to any argument above that you strongly disagree with. Make sure you focus on the religious dimensions of the issue you are discussing. For example, you might look at one of the following questions:

- How is sportsmanship a religious value?
- Is Grinnell "the least religious school in the country"?
- Is Jack Taylor a good representative for the Fellowship of Christian Athletes?
- Are sports simply games, or should they "mold character"?
- Is collegiate sport to be judged by a different standard for religiously affiliated schools?
- What factors might make blowouts morally justifiable?

CASE 15

Conclusion

WHAT WOULD PHIL JACKSON DO?

Fig. 15.1. Phil Jackson. AP Photo/Gaas.

GOAL: To pull together the concepts and ideas we have been examining by looking at the religious expression of Phil Jackson, NBA player, coach, executive, and "Zen master."

READ: Phil Jackson and Hugh Delehanty, *Sacred Hoops: Spiritual Lessons of a Hardwood Warrior* (New York: Hyperion, 1995).

I first learned to love professional basketball watching the New York Knicks in the early 1970s. I loved all of them—Frazier, Reed, Monroe, DeBusschere, Bradley; but my deepest affection was for "Action Jackson" as Phil was known back in those days. The sixth man, he would come off the bench and contribute a bit of chaos with his long arms, wild hair, and awkward movements. Jackson was a good basketball player, but it turned out he was a better coach; no longer known as Action Jackson, but rather nicknamed "The Zen Master," although he referred to himself as a Zen Christian. His story is a fitting conclusion to our examination of religion and sport.

Jackson is considered among the greatest coaches in NBA history, winning six championships with the Bulls and another five with the Los Angeles Lakers. His great strength and greatest challenge was turning individual stars like Michael Jordan, Kobe Bryant, and Shaquille O'Neal into players who valued team effort over individual success. According to Jackson, he was able to do this through bringing his understandings of religion to bear on basketball.

Jackson was raised in North Dakota by two Assemblies of God ministers who themselves had grown up Mennonite. He identified his father as the one who taught him love and compassion and his mother as the source of intellectual questioning. This gender "role reversal" allowed him to think about masculinity in ways that differed from social norms when and where he was growing up. He learned how to be a Christian from his family, strongly identifying with the message of Jesus's love and compassion. But he was uncomfortable with the part of his parents' faith that required memorizing Bible passages and adhering to rigid standards. And he found himself unable to "speak in tongues." Glossolalia, as it is known to scholars, is an experience of God speaking through you in sounds, as described in the New Testament (Acts 2:17). Pentecostals, like his parents, view it as a gift that recognizes your baptism in the Holy Spirit. Without access to this ritual Phil felt alienated. His parents did not permit television or movies, but believed that sports built character. Basketball (as well as football, baseball, and discus throwing) became escape valves for him in high school.

It was the sixties when Phil left home on a basketball scholarship to the University of North Dakota, and he played well enough for "The Fighting Sioux" to be drafted in the second round by the New York Knicks. During this era many young people were experimenting with different forms of spirituality. Phil's brother Joe started learning about other religions in college, became a Sufi (a practitioner of Islamic mysticism) and also dabbled in Zen Buddhism, to which he introduced Phil. Reading *Zen Mind, Beginner's Mind* by Shunryu Suzuki changed his life. Jackson recounts being impressed by the basic Buddhist ideas of giving up desire, paying attention to the present (even while doing mundane tasks), focusing on the collective and not the self, and understanding that everything is always changing. He learned the techniques of meditation, concentrating on the breath to focus attention and clear the mind. He understood Yogi Berra's insight that you can't think and hit at the same time in a new way.

Jackson was also affected by another book he read, William James's *Varieties of Religious Experience*. This text convinced him that religious wisdom was available from many traditions. The stories of the inner peace of Quakers, Shakers, and other Christian mystics convinced him that he didn't need drugs or speaking in tongues to be a good Christian himself; that quiet prayer could provide the inner peace he craved.

Jackson has one other nickname, "Swift Eagle," given to him when he and his Knick teammate Bill Bradley conducted basketball clinics on the Pine Ridge Reservation in South Dakota in the early 1970s. Bradley and Jackson volunteered to work with youth on the reservation because they were inspired by the Lakota's stance at Wounded Knee in 1973. A group of Lakota Indians who belonged to the American Indian Movement (AIM) occupied Wounded Knee, chosen for its symbolic value as the site of the 1890 massacre that ended the American Indian Wars and resulted in the deaths of over three hundred Lakota men, women, and children; AIM was protesting conditions on the reservation and the U.S. government's failure to honor its treaties with Native peoples.

Jackson was deeply impressed with Native spirituality, their profound respect for nature, and their belief that everything on the planet is sacred. Compelled by what he read in *Black Elk Speaks*, he admired the warrior vision, a willingness to make personal sacrifices for the betterment of the group, and the rituals that accompanied battles including chanting and the use of totems like arrows, owl feathers, tobacco pouches, white buffalo photos, and designating a location to make a sacred hoop before entering into battle.

It is the Lakota sacred hoop, not the one on the basketball court, that is the source of the title of Jackson's autobiography, focused on his experience coaching the Chicago Bulls to six NBA championships in the 1990s. Jackson explains how he used the lessons derived from Lakota traditions, Zen teachings, and Christian prayer to become an "invisible coach" who inspired a team to play selfless basketball through a Buddhist middle path of neither coddling his players nor letting them alone but finding a balance between supporting and respecting them. Jackson describes how he came to employ the triangle offense designed by his assistant coach, Tex Winter, as a means to realize a Zen approach. He describes the triangle as "five man tai chi," a Daoist principle that demands "yielding to your opponent's force in order to render him powerless."[1] The triangle involves all the players, rather than focusing on the one or two shooters, and gets all twelve players and the coaches to see themselves as an important part of a team, rather than focusing on their individual contributions. To succeed at this, they must all stay focused and be present in each moment. Jackson taught his players to quiet their minds through meditation, recited the Lord's Prayer with them, and created an inner sanctum adorned with Lakota symbols. At the beginning and at the end of practice they formed a sacred hoop to prepare themselves for the game.

ACTIVITIES

ACTIVITY 1

Respond to the following prompts: Watch the Audi advertisement Jackson made.[2] Is it in keeping with his philosophy? Why or why not? Does it fit with Jackson's views in *Sacred Hoops* about the commercialization of sport?

ACTIVITY 2

Watch Jackson's interview with Oprah Winfrey.[3] Are Jackson's techniques performance enhancement? Why or why not? Compare Jackson's understanding of being in the moment with the concept of flow.

ACTIVITY 3

Jackson has been criticized for his appropriation of Native and Buddhist rituals. Is Jackson's use of these techniques acceptable in the context of sports? Imagine that you are a religious practitioner or a member of one of Jackson's sports teams. Write Jackson a letter explaining why you are or are not comfortable with his use of religious rituals.

CONCLUDING ACTIVITIES

Activity 1a

Answer the question "What would Phil Jackson do?" in response to the cases you have encountered in this text. For each prompt that follows, explain how you think Phil Jackson would respond to the situation. In each case provide a quotation from *Sacred Hoops*, either Jackson's own words or one of the epigraphs he chooses to start each chapter. Explain why you chose that quote to represent Jackson's thoughts on the matter. Note: you may not use the same quote more than twice.

What would Phil Jackson do (or say)

- if he were asked to comment about whether high school football was the religion of Odessa, Texas?

- if he were asked to comment on whether Oscar Pistorius had an unfair advantage running on "cheetah legs"?
- if he were asked to write a preface for Eugen Herrigel's *Zen in the Art of Archery?*
- if Julie Byrne asked him to provide a blurb for *O God of Players?*
- if the press asked him to compare his meditation techniques with juju practices in African football?
- if the commissioner of baseball asked his advice about how to handle the problems between Baseball Chapel and Jewish umpires?
- if he were a Jewish Olympian and selected to participate in the 1936 games in Berlin?
- if congregants of Temple Beth El asked him whether Bishop Plummer did the right thing in quitting Negro League baseball?
- if he were Mahmoud Abdul-Rauf's coach and Abdul-Rauf told him he would no longer be standing with the team for the playing of the national anthem?
- if he were invited by the International Olympic Committee to help adjudicate the controversy over women wrestling in hijab?
- if Archbishop Chaput asked his opinion about whether girls should be allowed to continue playing football on Philadelphia CYO teams?
- if a representative of PETA wrote to tell him that his fame and his status as the former coach of the Chicago "Bulls" made him a really important person to ask the pope to condemn the San Fermin festival?
- if he were asked to take sides on the Florida State mascot controversy?
- if he were Jack Taylor responding to media criticism that he was a "ball hog"?

Activity 1b

Pick three from the list where you disagree with his position and explain to Jackson why you would choose a different solution to the problem.

Activity 2

Write a response to one of the difficult issues in sports today that we did not cover this semester (for example, concussions, gambling, the politics of race, or athletes coming out as gay). What would Phil Jackson do about these issues? What would you do?

NOTES

A Note to Instructors on How to Use This Text

1. Common texts are William J. Baker, *Playing with God: Religion and Modern Sports* (Cambridge: Harvard University Press, 2007); Andrew Cooper, *Playing in the Zone: Exploring the Spiritual Dimensions of Sports* (Boston: Shambhala, 1998); Craig Forney, *The Holy Trinity of American Sports: Civil Religion in Football, Baseball, and Basketball* (Macon, GA: Mercer University Press, 2010); Allen Guttmann, *From Ritual to Record: The Nature of Modern Sports* (New York: Columbia University Press, 1978); Shirl J. Hoffman, *Good Game: Christianity and the Culture of Sports* (Waco, TX: Baylor University Press, 2010); Tara Magdalinski and Timothy J. L. Chandler, eds., *With God on Their Side: Sport in the Service of Religion* (New York: Routledge, 2002); Michael Novak, *The Joy of Sports: Endzones, Bases, Baskets, Balls, and the Consecration of the American Spirit* (New York: Basic Books, 1976); Charles Prebish, *Religion and Sport: The Meeting of Sacred and Profane* (Westport, CT: Greenwood, 1993); Joseph Price, *From Season to Season: Sport as American Religion* (Macon, GA: Mercer University Press, 2001); Jeffrey Scholes and Raphael Sassower, *Religion and Sports in American Culture* (New York: Routledge, 2014); Nick J. Watson and Andrew Parker, *Sports and Christianity: Historical and Contemporary Perspectives* (New York: Routledge, 2013).

Case 3. Zen and Archery in Japan

1. See Allen Guttmann, *From Ritual to Record: The Nature of Modern Sports* (New York: Columbia University Press, 2004).

2. John Stevens, who considered himself a disciple of Awa, believed that he was teaching in the tradition of Zen and didn't intend to start a new religion. See John Stevens, *Zen Bow, Zen Arrow: The Life and Teachings of Awa Kenzo, the Archery Master from Zen in the Art of Archery* (Boston: Shambhala, 2007).

3. Eugen Herrigel, *Zen in the Art of Archery* (New York: Pantheon, 1953).

4. See the exhaustive list that appears as appendix C (59–70) in R. John Williams, "Technê-Zen and the Spiritual Quality of Global Capitalism," *Critical Inquiry* 38.1 (Autumn 2011): 17–70.

5. Shoji Yamada first published his insights in an article, "The Myth of Zen in the Art of Archery," *Japanese Journal of Religious Studies* 28:1–2 (2001): 1–31. Yamada develops these insights further in *Shots in the Dark: Japan, Zen, and the West* (Chicago: University of Chicago Press; Kyoto: International Research Center for Japanese Studies, 2009). Some scholars like Arthur Koestler, "A Stink of Zen," *Encounter* (October 1960): 13–32, had previously noted this as an issue.

6. See Gershom Scholem, "Zen-Nazism?" *Encounter* (February 1961): 96.

7. "On Target: Columbia's Archer Has a Yen for Zen and Becoming No. 1," *Newsday*, February 21, 1988, accessed at http://search.proquest.com.libproxy.temple.edu /docview/277968364?accountid=14270.

8. "Getting to the Point Kyudo Archers Meet in East L.A. Not So Much to Hit Targets, but to 'Shoot Themselves' with Discipline," *Los Angeles Times,* March 28, 1993, accessed at http://search.proquest.com/docview/281917932?accountid =14270.

9. Stevens, *Zen Bow, Zen Arrow,* 14.

CASE 5. JUJU

1. As my colleague Terry Rey reminded me, "The sense of the word *juju* is evocative of what many English speakers might superficially or intuitively understand by the word 'voodoo,' which should not be confused with the Afro-Caribbean religion of Haitian origins known as Vodou."

2. The exception to this rule is the work of E. E. Evans-Pritchard in his remarkable study of witchcraft in Central Africa, *Witchcraft, Oracles and Magic Among the Azande* (Oxford: Clarendon, 1937) where he demonstrates the rational and logical nature of these practices.

3. See Peter Geschiere, *The Modernity of Witchcraft: Politics and the Occult in Postcolonial Africa* (Charlottesville: University of Virginia Press, 1997), 4. In a footnote he comments: "Soccer more or less replaced the ancient practices of *doomb* (war) between the villages. As in the old *doomb*, the support of the occult forces was seen as an indispensable condition for victory" (226, note 6).

4. Onochie Anibeze, "Nwanu Laments Africa's Juju Stories," *Africa News Service,* June 20, 2006; *Business Insights: Global,* June 24, 2013 http://business.highbeam. com/3548/article-1G1-147256769/nwanu-laments-africa-juju-stories.

5. I found stories that described juju ceremonies and rituals practiced in the following countries: Ghana, Nigeria, Togo, Kenya, South Africa, Tanzania, Zimbabwe, Cameroon, Benin, Malawi, Gambia, Rwanda, Uganda, Congo, Senegal, Mali, Burkina Faso, Democratic Republic of the Congo, Mozambique, Côte d'Ivoire, and Swaziland.

6. Dawn Starin, "Welcome to Gambian Football," *New African* 480 (January 2009): 62–63.

7. Anouk Zijlma, "Voodoo, Black Magic, Juju, Obeah . . . " January 19, 2012. Accessed at http://goafrica.about.com/b/2012/01/19/voodoo-black-magic-juju -obeah.htm.

8. Marc Lacey, "It's a New Season for Soccer Sorcerers," *Toronto Star*, August 11, 2002.

9. "Of Durban, Raw Eggs, Juju and Football," AllAfrica.com, February 21, 2013.

10. "Over-Reliance on Witchcraft Reduces Soccer to Occultism," *Taipei Times,* June 28, 2009. Accessed at http://www.taipeitimes.com/News/sport/archives /2009/06/28/2003447315.

11. Jonathan Wilson, "What You Need to Know to Watch the African Cup of Nations," *Financial Times*, January 19, 2008.

12. "Magic Fails to Help Cameroon's Footballers," January 2012, http://www.bbc .co.uk/news/world-africa-16471695. Geschiere explains that "visiting teams often prefer to stay at a mission station—in particular, with European missionaries—because the Christian religion and the 'magic of the white man' offers at least some sort of protection against occult aggression" (4).

13. "Congo Soccer Riot Over 'Witchcraft' Leaves 13 Dead," September 15, 2008. Accessed at: http://espnfc.com/news/story?id=572469&sec=world&cc=5901.

14. "Getting the Black Stars Ready for Can 2012—Juju in Black Stars Camp?" *Africa News Service,* October 21, 2011; *Business Insights: Global,* June 24, 2013, http:// bi.galegroup.com.libproxy.temple.edufglobaVarticle/GALE%7CA270355430 /aef6b9e4eefob06619f697edfec12ebt7.

15. Thilo Thielke, "They'll Put a Spell on You: The Witchdoctors of African Football," June 11, 2010. Accessed at http://www.spiegel.de/international/zeitgeist/they-ll -put-a-spell-on-you-the-witchdoctors-of-african-football-a-699704.html.

16. "Football: Hot Shots Six to Follow in Burkina Faso," *Guardian,* February 6, 1998.

17. Leo Igwe, "Witchcraft and African Football." Accessed at http://www.ghanaweb .com/GhanaHomePage/SportsArchive/artikel.php?ID=264004.

18. Stephan Lovgren, "World Cup Witchcraft: Africa Teams Turn to Magic for Aid," *National Geographic News,* June 30, 2006.

19. "Use of Juju Makes No News at All," June 12, 2011. Accessed at www.allafrica.com.

20. Davan Maharaj, "African Soccer Teams Rely On Medicine Men to Ward Off Evil Spirits and Enemy Shots, to the Dismay of Some Game Administrators," *Los Angeles Times*, May 31, 2002.

21. Susannah Herbert, "Out of This World at the World Cup: African Teams Have Brought a Fetishist (for Goalkeepers), Rams (for Slaughter) and Candles (for Jinxing Foes)," *Vancouver Sun,* June 11, 1998.

Case 6. Jewish Umpires and Baseball Chapel

1. "In Baseball Now More Teams Pray Before They Play," *Washington Post*, September 18, 2005.

2. Alan Cooperman, "Nats' Church Apologizes for Remarks About Jews," *Washington Post*, September 21, 2005.

3. Alan Cooperman, "MLB Is Reviewing Baseball Chapel; Evangelical Group Concerns Selig" *Washington Post*, October 1, 2005.

4. Karin Tanabe, "Is the Nation's Favorite Pastime Pitching Jesus?" *Moment* 32.5 (October/November 2007): 38–45, 60–65, 69.

5. Ari Sunshine, "It's Time to End Baseball's Religious Monopoly," *Washington Jewish Week*, October 18, 2007.

6. Quoted in Murray Chass, "Should a Clubhouse Be a Chapel?" *New York Times,* February 2, 2008.

7. A biography of Spoelstra by Benjamin Hoak can be accessed at http://www.worldji.com/resources/view/45.

8. Baseball Chapel declined permission to include an image of their logo in this book, but you can find it and much more information about the organization at www.baseballchapel.org.

9. Hank Hersch, "The Gospel and Gaetti," *Sports Illustrated*, August 21, 1989.

10. Daniel Okrent, *Nine Innings: The Anatomy of a Baseball Game* (Boston: Houghton Mifflin, 2000), 95.

11. www.baseballchapel.org.

Case 7. American Jews and the Boycott of the 1936 Berlin Olympics

1. "Sherrill Rebuffs Olympic Ban Plea; Scores Agitation," *New York Times*, October 22, 1935.

2. Accessed at http://wymaninstitute.org/press/2008-8-11.php.

CASE 8. THE BELLEVILLE GRAYS AND PLAYING SPORTS
ON THE SABBATH

1. See Leslie A. Heaphy, *The Negro Leagues, 1869–1960* (Jefferson, NC: McFarland, 2003) for a comprehensive picture of the many leagues that were formed during the course of black baseball history.

2. Lawrence W. Levine, *Black Culture and Black Consciousness: Afro-American Folk Thought from Slavery to Freedom* (New York: Oxford University Press, 1977), 50; Albert J. Raboteau, *Slave Religion: The "Invisible Institution" in the Antebellum South* (New York: Oxford University Press, 1980), 33; Katherine Dvorak, "After Apocalypse, Moses," in John B. Boles, *Masters and Slaves in the House of the Lord: Race and Religion in the American South, 1740–1870* (Lexington: University Press of Kentucky, 1988), 175.

3. Raboteau, *Slave Religion*, 109; *1906 Census of Religious Bodies*, 202. The Holy Kiss was abandoned when it brought censure for sexuality.

4. Church of God and Saints of Christ, and Historical Committee, *History of the Church of God and Saints of Christ* (Suffolk, VA: The Church, 1992), 39–44.

5. I witnessed these practices at Sabbath services in Belleville and Philadelphia and gleaned information from conversations with community members, the church history, and their Web site, www.cogasoc.org. Many of their practices are reminiscent of classical Reform Judaism, including the interchangeable use of Hebrew and Israelite as terms of identification, recitation of the Lord's Prayer, and collection taking. Norfolk *Journal and Guide* (NJG), April 26, 1951.

6. Historical Committee, *History*, 48–50; Oral histories conducted by the author with members of the Belleville community, June 2008.

7. *Pittsburgh Courier* (PC), March 6, 1932; Thomas Burt, former Negro League player, face-to-face interview with author, June 2008.

8. Joel Wagner, face-to-face conversation with author, June 2008; NJG, July 23, 1932.

9. NJG, May 7, July 23, and September 3, 1932; Buck Leonard and James A. Riley. *Buck Leonard: The Black Lou Gehrig: The Hall of Famer's Story in His Own Words* (New York: Carroll & Graf, 1995), 18–19.

10. NJG, July 16, 1938.

11. NJG, June 16, July 2, July 16, August 20, September 3, September 10, 1938.

12. NJG, July 16, 1938; letter from John B. Johnson to Abe Manley, August 3, 1938, *Newark Eagle* Papers (NEP), Newark Public Library; NJG, August 27, 1938.

13. *Chicago Defender* (CD), June 13, 1936; Alfred M., and Alfred T. Martin. *The Negro Leagues in New Jersey: A History* (Jefferson, NC: McFarland, 2008), 65–66.

14. CD and *Afro-American* (AA), January 28, 1939; Art Carter, "From the Bench," AA, February 18, 1939; Baltimore AA, February 25, 1939; *New York Amsterdam News* (NYAN), March 11, 1939.

15. Letter from John B. Johnson to Mr. and Mrs. Abe Manley, February 3, 1939, and to Abe Manley, February 25, 1939, NEP; Sam Lacy, Richmond, AA, May 6, 1939.

16. NJG, May 27, 1939; D. E. Ellis, "Cruising Along the Baseball Front with the ECL," *New York Age* (NYA), May 27, 1939.

17. NJG, May 13, 1939, June 8, 1940; NYAN, March 29, 1947, and March 11, 1950; NYA, May 10, 1939.

18. Sam Lacy, Baltimore, AA, June 3, 1939.

19. NJG, June 10, 1939; NYA, June 24, 1939.

20. Darrell J. Howard, *"Sunday Coming": Black Baseball in Virginia* (Jefferson, NC: McFarland, 2002), 25.

21. NJG, July 1, 1939; Telegram from Brady Johnson to Abe Manley, August 2, 1939, NEP.

22. Art Carter to "Mr. L. Z. Plummer, The Bellevue Grays,[sic] Portsmouth, Va., March 28, 1940, Art Carter Papers, Moorland Spingarn Research Library, Howard University; Richmond, AA, April 13, 1940.

23. NJG, May 18, 1940; Letter from Art Carter to Joe Lewis, May 30, 1940; Letter from Art Carter to H. Z. Plummer, June 8, 1940; Art Carter to Joe Miles, June 10, 1940, Carter Papers.

24. Richmond, AA, July 20, 1940; Telegram from Joe Lewis to Art Carter, July 10, 1940; Letter from Art Carter to Joe Miles, August 23, 1940, Carter Papers.

25. PC, June 8, 1940.

CASE 9. MAHMOUD ABDUL-RAUF AND THE NATIONAL ANTHEM RITUAL IN THE NBA

1. Robert Sanchez, "The Conversion of Chris Jackson," *5280 Denver Magazine* (October 2007).

2. "Statement by Mahmoud Abdul-Rauf on Anthem," AP News Archive (March 13, 1996). Accessed at http://www.apnewsarchive.com/1996/Statement-by -Mahmoud-Abdul-Rauf-on-Anthem/id-9294cd3a18cac6bb0c80aba84863ade9.

3. "A Puzzled Olajuwon Speaks Out on Citizenship," *New York Times*, March 14, 1996.

4. "Playing by the Rules," Online News Hour PBS (March 14, 1996). Accessed at http://www.pbs.org/newshour/bb/sports/nba_debate_3-14.html.

5. Reported by Peter Steinfels, "Anthems, Islam and Basketball," *New York Times*, March 17, 1996.

6. William Brown, "Abdul-Rauf, Mahmoud," in Edward E. Curtis IV, ed., *Encyclopedia of Muslim-American History* (New York: Facts On File, 2010).

7. Kelly B. Koenig, "Mahmoud Abdul-Rauf's Suspension for Refusing to Stand for the National Anthem: A 'Free Throw' for the NBA and Denver Nuggets, or a 'Slam Dunk' Violation of Abdul-Rauf's Title Vii Rights?" *Washington University Law Quarterly* 76 (1998): 377–405.

8. See http://www.youtube.com/watch?v=SZoYTmb76bY.

CASE 10. JUDO AND HIJAB AT THE OLYMPICS

1. Tansin Benn, Gertrud Pfister, and Haifaa Jawad, eds., *Muslim Women and Sport* (New York: Routledge, 2011), 34.

2. You can see these designs at the Web site of the Hijab Shop, http://www.the hijabshop.com/capsters/index.php.

3. Accessed at http://www.ijf.org/, 91–113.

4. Campbell Robertson, "82 Seconds, Long Enough For History," August 4, 2012, http://www.nytimes.com/2012/08/04/sports/Olympics/wojdan-shaherkani -first-female-saudi-olympian-loses-in-debut.html?_r=0. You can see the Associated Press images and a report on the match here: http://www.youtube.com /watch?v=JU49kttKhKE.

5. Two quotes above, David Whitley, "Muslim Woman Will Compete for Saudi Arabia in Judo . . . with a Hijab," July 31, 2012, http://www.sportingnews.com /Olympics/story/2012-07-31/olympics-2012-muslim-woman-judo-hijab -saudi-arabia-islamic-dress-london-summer-g.

6. Three quotes above, Mark Sappenfield, "Saudi Olympic Athlete Hit by Judo Head Scarf Ban: Safety or Discrimination?" July 27, 2012, accessed at http:// www.csmonitor.com/World/Olympics/2012/0727/Saudi-Olympic-athlete-hit -by-judo-head-scarf=ban-Safety-or-discrimination-video.

CASE 11. CAROLINE PLA AND CYO FOOTBALL

1. Chris Palmer, "Passing Downfield to Another Girl," *Philadelphia Inquirer,* February 25, 2013.

2. You will find this petition at https://www.change.org/petitions/let-girls-play -football-stop-the-discrimination-by-the-archdiocese-of-philadelphia-cyo -office.

3. Christina Settimi, "Caroline Pla, 11-Year Old Football Player, Discriminated Against By the Catholic Church," *Forbes Magazine*, January 11, 2013.

4. Larry Mendte, "Bucks' Caroline Pla Didn't Get Banned from CYO Football Because She's a Girl," *Philadelphia Magazine,* January 10, 2013. Accessed at http://blogs.phillymag .com/the_philly_post/2013/01/10/pennsylvania-caroline-pla-banned-football-girl/.

5. Charles Martin Cosgriff, "Caroline Pla Does Not Have the Right to Play CYO Football," January 9, 2013. Accessed at http://www.examiner.com/article/caroline-pla-does-not-have-the-right-to-play-cyo-football.
6. See http://www.youtube.com/watch?v=VJWKEFY7XhQ.
7. Quoted in Settimi, "Caroline Pla, 11-Year Old Football Player."

CASE 12. SHOULD THE ROMAN CATHOLIC CHURCH CONDEMN BULLFIGHTING IN SPAIN?

1. You can find a translation at http://es.wikisource.org/wiki/De_salutis_gregi_Dominici.
2. See Adrian Shubert, *Death and Money in the Afternoon: a History of the Spanish Bullfight* (New York: Oxford University Press, 1999), chapter 5.
3. Ernest Hemingway, *Death in the Afternoon* (New York: Scribner's, 1932), 16.
4. Shubert, *Death and Money in the Afternoon.*
5. http://www.sharkonline.org/?P=0000000423.
6. "Moment of Truth," posted anonymously, n.d. Accessed at http://www.stopbullfighting.org.uk/moment_of_truth.htm.
7. Ibid.
8. Kenneth Tynan, *Bull Fever* (New York: Atheneum, 1966), 10.
9. Matilda Mench, *Life on the Line: the Heroic Story of Vicki Moore* (Liverpool: Bluecoat, 2007), 78.
10. Hemingway, *Death in the Afternoon,* 232–233.
11. Mench, *Life on the Line,* 78.

CASE 13. THE FLORIDA STATE UNIVERSITY SEMINOLES' OSCEOLA AND RENEGADE

1. See www.fsu.edu.
2. Accessed at http://www.tallahasseeseminoleclub.com/FSU%20Traditions.
3. S. L. Price, "The Indian Wars," *Sports Illustrated*, March 4, 2002.
4. Accessed at http://blogs.orlandosentinel.com/sports_college_fsu/2011/07/florida-state-wins-espn-sportsnation-traditions-poll.html.

CASE 14. JACK TAYLOR'S 138 POINTS

1. Mickey Seward, "Higher Score: Taylor Aims to Glorify Christ," Fellowship of Christian Athletes Web site, December 19, 2012. Accessed at http://

www.fca.org/2012/12/19/higher-score-jack-taylor-aims-to-glorify-christ/#.UfkSQI3OkxE.

2. "History and Philosophy," NCCAA Web site. Accessed at http://www.thenccaa.org/sports/2012/5/7/about_us.aspx.

3. Jesse Temple, "How Do You Allow 138 Points to One Player?" Fox Sports Wisconsin Web site, November 21, 2012. Accessed at http://www.foxsportswisconsin.com/11/21/12/The-real-question-How-do-you-allow-138-p/landing.html?blockID=823903.

4. Quoted in Samuel G. Freedman, "A Basketball Blowout and Its Celebration Raise Theological Questions," *New York Times*, April 5, 2013.

5. www.grinnell.edu.

6. Hemant Mehta, "Faith Baptist Bible College on the Losing End of a Record Shattering Basketball Performance," November 21, 2012. Accessed at http://www.patheos.com/blogs/friendlyatheist/2012/11/21/faith-baptist-bible-college-on-the-losing-end-of-a-record-shattering-basketball-performance/. It is interesting to observe how liberal religious values are often assumed to be "atheist" in our contemporary culture, which equates religion with fundamentalism.

7. Liam Day, "There Is Never an Excuse for Embarrassing an Opponent: Grinnell vs. Faith Baptist," November 22, 2012. Accessed at http://goodmenproject.com/good-feed-blog/there-is-never-an-excuse-for-embarrassing-an-opponent-grinnell-vs-faith-baptist/.

8. Quoted in Freedman, "A Basketball Blowout and Its Celebration."

9. Joe Carter, "Why You Should Always Run Up the Score," *First Things* Web site, January 26, 2011. Accessed at http://www.firstthings.com/blogs/firstthoughts/2011/01/26/why-you-should-always-run-up-the-score/.

10. Joshua Hess, "Running Up the Score—a Jewish Perspective," The FANatic Rabbi, November 18, 2010. Accessed at http://thefanaticrabbi.com/2010/11/running-score-jewish-perspective/#sthash.8aGze3y8.dpuf.

11. David Arsenault, *The Running Game: A Formula for Success* (Spring City, PA: Reedswain, 1997).

12. Doug Cutchins, "In Defense of 138," Grinnell College Web site, November 28, 2012. Accessed at http://www.grinnell.edu/news/releases/defense-138.

13. Nicholas Dixon, "On Sportsmanship and 'Running Up the Score,'" *Journal of the Philosophy of Sport* 19 (1992): 1–13.

14. Randolph Feezel, *Sport, Play and Ethical Reflection* (Urbana: University of Illinois Press, 2004), 111–122.

15. "Is Running Up the Score a Problem?" November 17, 2010. ESPN.com. Accessed at http://espn.go.com/espn/print?id=5816279&type=story.

16. See http://www.youtube.com/watch?v=bQ9zKNQKwuw.

CASE 15. CONCLUSION

1. Phil Jackson and Hugh Delehanty, *Sacred Hoops: Spiritual Lessons of a Hardwood Warrior* (New York: Hyperion, 1995), 136.

2. See http://www.youtube.com/watch?v=vVr02KGMjRM.

3. See http://www.huffingtonpost.com/2013/07/17/phil-jackson-meditation-coaching-tactics_n_3606632.html.

INDEX